RAZING PALESTINE

RAZING PALESTINE

PUNISHING SOLIDARITY AND DISSENT IN CANADA

Edited by

LEILA MARSHY

Baraka Books

Montréal

ISBN paper 9781771863957 | ePub 9781771864176 |
PDF 9781771864183

Cover design: Samia Marshy
Cover photo: republished with the express permission of Calgary Herald, a division of Postmedia Network Inc.
Editing: Elise Moser
Proofreading: Anne Marie Marko
Book design: Folio infographie

Legal Deposit, 4th quarter 2025
Bibliothèque et Archives nationales du Québec
Library and Archives Canada

Published by Baraka Books of Montreal
Printed and bound in Quebec by Imprimerie Gauvin

TRADE DISTRIBUTION AND RETURNS
Canada: UTPdistribution.com | USA: IPGbook.com

We acknowledge the support from the Société de développement des entreprises culturelles (SODEC) and the Government of Quebec tax credit for book publishing administered by SODEC.

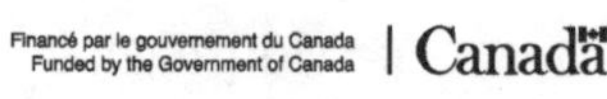

Table of contents

PART TWO: RADIO SILENCE

PART THREE: NO IVORY TOWER

FOREWORD

We Must Be Allowed to Speak Out

Gabor Maté, MD, CM

This anthology is subversive in the most positive sense of the word. It seeks to provide an unequivocal and evidence-based response to the enforced silence around what millions of people the world over recognize as the most urgent moral issue of our time: the unspeakable suffering imposed on the people of Gaza, a suffering ignored or minimized and even justified throughout our media, political strata and educational institutions. In other words, it subverts the subversion of truth.

Much of that imposition of silence occurs in the name of combatting antisemitism. While real enough, all too real as a heinous ideology, these days antisemitism is also at times a phantasm, a specter evoked to intimidate people from expressing their grief, outrage, and demands for justice. It is essential that people of conscience—Jews, non-Jews, all of us—strive to make that crucial distinction. The costs of failing to do so are devastating. Devastating for human lives in the Middle East, and devastating, too, for the moral and psychic well-being of many others, including here in Canada.

"The IDF [Israel Defense Forces] of the past 20 months is an army of slaughter like the world has never seen. An army paving the way for genocide and population transfer... It destroys and takes pride, kills and preens." So writes the intrepid Israeli journalist Gideon Levy in a recent column.[1]

Harsh words? If so, Levy is far from alone. Renowned Israeli scholars of genocide have found that their country's actions in Gaza meet the international legal definition of that felony. A widely circulated petition by over 1300 Israeli academics[2] denounces what they term "this horrifying litany of war crimes and crimes against humanity... We cannot claim we did not know. We have been silent for too long." Former Israeli prime minister Ehud Olmert acknowledged,[3] "Yes, Israel is committing war crimes." IDF reserve major general Yair Golan, leader of the Democratic party in the Knesset, has accused Israeli forces in Gaza of killing babies "for a hobby."[4]

We could learn from such salutary bluntness, for in Canada similar openness is heavily discouraged. In this country, voicing like opinions would immediately draw—has drawn—charges of antisemitic "blood libel," or, if uttered by Jews like me, of coming from self-hating supporters of terror. In the health care field, my own domain of work,[5] people have lost their jobs[6] or have been threatened with professional disqualification[7] for saying far less. Statements pointing to Israel's oppressive and lethal actions are portrayed as slanderous, beyond the pale of reasoned commentary. They make some Jewish people feel singled out and "unsafe," is the usual complaint. I know of no cases of medical personnel being harassed over exercising their democratic right to support Israeli policy.

Just as nothing justifies the atrocities of October 7, nothing about October 7 justifies Israeli atrocities against the Palestinians, either before or since October 7. Recently, I listened to orthopedic surgeon Dr. Deirdre Nunan, like me a graduate of UBC's Faculty of Medicine, recount her harrowing experiences serving in a Gaza hospital under the siege that followed Israel's breaking of the ceasefire in March. Her depictions of unspeakable horror, enacted as policy by one of the world's most sophisticated militaries, were soul shattering. Many other physicians—Canadian, American, Jewish, Muslim, Christian—who have worked in Gaza speak in similar terms. British doctors describe witnessing "a slaughterhouse." All their testimonies are widely accessible. The leading medical journal *Lancet* editorialized that in its assault on health care facilities and personnel in Gaza, "the Israeli Government has acted with impunity... Many medical academies and health professional organizations that claim a commitment to social justice have failed to speak out."[8]

As if to illustrate that lament, a letter by a group of us concerned physicians, several of us Jewish, to the *British Columbia Medical Journal* decrying the offensive against Gaza's health system, was refused. It failed to meet the *Journal*'s "criteria," we were told. It both appalled and pained us that the urgency of drawing attention to the large-scale and deliberate targeting, killing, and torture of our Palestinian health colleagues—with the evident complicity of the Israeli medical establishment[9]—was not deemed sufficient to warrant publication. Dr. Adnan

Al-Bursh, for example, head of orthopedics at Gaza's Al-Shifa hospital, was a dedicated surgeon, athlete, and the father of five. In what moral universe or realm of professional ethics is it not the immediate and compelling concern of every medical body and institution on the planet that this vigorous 51-year-old, abducted from work, died in torment after being "processed" for five months in Israel's notorious detention centres?

I am well familiar with antisemitism. Growing up in postwar Hungary I was often confronted with it as, for example, when being attacked by a group voicing Jew-baiting slogans. I had a friend come to my defence. "Leave him alone," he chided the bullies, "it's not his fault he is Jewish." "Great," it struck me—"a fault, but at least not mine."

It may be true that antisemitic animus can lurk behind critiques of Zionism. But in my decades of advocacy for Palestinian rights including medical visits to Gaza and the West Bank, I have rarely witnessed it. When present, it has a certain tone that one can feel is directed at Jewishness itself, rather than at the theory and practice of Zionism or at Israel's actions. What is far more common and genuinely confusing for many is that Israel and its supporters, Jews and non-Jews, habitually confound opposition to Israeli policy with antisemitism. This is akin to Vietnam War protesters being accused of anti-Americanism. How is opposing the napalming of human beings anti-American or, say, deploring Israel's use of mass starvation as a weapon of war in any sense anti-Jewish?

The effect is that many are terrified to speak out. No one wants to be associated with one of the most noxious ideologies in history and people also genuinely fear being ostracized. I meet such people everywhere. Their hearts anguished, their lips remain tight. "I am outraged; I have nightmares. I feel completely helpless," one woman told me. "It's distressing, every day." "As a Jew I'm appalled at what Israel is doing," the head of a leading Canadian cultural organization avowed in a private conversation, "but I have many employees. I cannot jeopardize their jobs."

Many suffer what has been called "moral injury," a mental state that occurs "under stressful circumstances, [when] people may perpetrate, fail to prevent, or witness events that contradict deeply held moral beliefs and expectations." It's disturbing to experience, accompanied by a sense of inertness and shame.

The only resolution is the freeing of the discussion around Gaza. People deserve the right to experience as much liberty to publicly mourn, question, oppose, deplore, denounce what they perceive as the perpetration of injustice and inhumanity as they do, in this country, to advocate for the aims and actions of the Israeli government and its Canadian abettors amongst our political leadership, academia, and media.

Even if we feel powerless to stop the first genocide we have ever watched on our screens in real time, allow at least our hearts to be broken openly, as mine is. And more, let us be free to take democratic, non-hateful action without fear of incurring the calumny of racism.

Notes

1. Gideon Levy, "Millions of Israelis Still Believe it is Obligatory to Love the IDF," *Ha'aretz*, 4 June 2025.
2. Avner Wishnitzer, "Black Flag: An Urgent Call to the Heads of Academia in Israel, signed by more than 1400 academics," *ResearchGate*, May 2025.
3. Ehud Omert, "Enough is Enough. Israel Is Committing War Crimes," *Ha'aretz*, 27 May 2025.
4. Thomas Friedman and Patrick Healy, "Tom Friedman on Why Life is Getting Much, Much Harder for Benjamin Netanyahu," *The New York Times*, 29 May 2025.
5. See this volume, "Two Letters", Yipeng Ge.

Arthur White-Crummy, "Doctor suspended from U of O residency after pro-Palestinian social media posts," *CBC News*, 21 November 2023.

6. Jason Proctor, "Northern Health defends handling of complaints over director's pro-Palestinian statements," *CBC News*, 19 November 2024.
7. Judy Trinh, "Ontario doctors disciplined over Israel-Gaza Protests," *CTV News*, 29 November 2023.
8. "Gaza has been failed by silence and impunity," *The Lancet*, 24 May 2025.
9. Neve Gordon, Guy Shalev, Osama Tanous, "The Shame of Israeli Medicine," *The New York Review*, 31 May 2025.

INTRODUCTION

Naked Emperor

Leila Marshy

If we've learned anything since October 2023, it is how much is invested in ensuring Israel faces no real consequences. Business goes on as usual, governments avert their gazes, mainstream media contorts itself to avoid saying a thing is a thing, and the accusation of antisemitism hovers over every discussion, action, and political position.

Dozens of UN resolutions since 1948 haven't stopped Israel. Oslo 1993 only furthered West Bank bantustanization. Decades of reports by Amnesty International, Médecins sans frontières, Human Rights Watch, and the UN—corroborated by the US State Department and Israeli NGOs—achieved nothing. Canada shunned UN Special Rapporteur Francesca Albanese. And the International Court of Justice (ICJ) was sidelined for declaring the emperor naked. Its 2024 genocide ruling was simply ignored by Israel and the United States, with the latter applying sanctions to South Africa who brought the case forward. Other Western countries, including Canada, refused to support the ruling.

What are world leaders telling us? They are telling us that Israel's geopolitical position trumps everything.

Whatever harrowing images emerge from Gaza, Israel matters more. They endorse Israel's "right to exist" predicated on 70-plus years of apartheid and brutality—and, currently, in spite of the charred babies, machine-gunned children, massacred doctors, assassinated journalists, incinerated hospitals, phalanxes of quadcopters called SMASH Dragons, and bulldozers burying people alive.[1] Not to mention, a death toll *The Lancet* medical journal estimates to be in the hundreds of thousands.[2] Israel's right to exist justifies and sanctions it all. My clothes are the finest silk, Israel says, and around the world a coterie of yes men, yes governments, and yes media nod and pretend to touch the shimmering fabric.

But people stepped into this moral void, and watched a genocide unfold in real time. And the power of social media emerged almost immediately. Israeli October 7 lies, parroted by mainstream outlets, were systematically debunked. On TikTok, as IDF soldiers danced in bloodied lingerie, Palestinian accounts exposed propaganda masquerading as history. Gazan journalists captured imaginations—nine-year-old Lama Jamous reporting while fleeing crisis to crisis; Bisan Owda's daily "It's Bisan from Gaza and I'm still alive" earning a 2024 Peabody Award for news; poet Rifaat Elareer becoming a household name with "If I should die." And then dying.

Many Canadians connected Indigenous erasure here with Palestinian erasure there. We don't hide our settler colonial past anymore—some of us attempt to find both Truth and Reconciliation, commemorate Missing and Murdered Indigenous Women, promise No Child Left Behind, acknowledge Land Back. While we can't undo the horrors or bring back the Beothuk, history compels us to make amends and move forward together. Spilled Indigenous blood remains a permanent tattoo, a reminder, a cautionary tale.

Unsurprisingly, Canadian institutions cracked down on pro-Palestinian protesters—a move familiar to those remembering Oka 1990, Ipperwash and Gustafson Lake 1995, Idle No More 2012, Wet'suwet'en 2019. As always, the same institutions upholding democratic values enforce silence and punish dissent.

Just as Justin Trudeau refused to call Indigenous destruction "genocide," he avoided the term for Gaza, and took 14 long months to demand a ceasefire. Prime Minister Mark Carney can barely condemn Israel's "unwillingness to prevent humanitarian disaster"—as if it were an oversight, not policy. He goes on to promise a two-state solution like it's a panacea for what ails us. But two things: (i) the vast majority of countries around the world have been supporting a two-state solution for 20 years; and (ii) Israel is pledging no Palestine by this time next year. "We will bury the idea of a Palestinian state," said Israeli minister Smotrich in August, 2025.[3]

The Canadian government, like others, won't declare the emperor naked. They won't admit that rather than silk, the only thing in their hands is the texture of power, the weave of compromise, and the fear of their complicity unravelling for all to see.

Political is Always Personal

This is a personal book. It's not a novel or short stories, but "political" books aren't impersonal—they reflect lived experiences, research, midnight revelations, confrontations, missed connections, hard truths, forged community, trauma, joy, hope.

It's personal because truth-telling's cost isn't just lost careers, but childhood fear when my father spoke about Palestine in Montreal. Threats escalating from phone calls to stalking to rocks—like clockwork whenever he addressed churches, synagogues, or newspapers, trying to "insert humanity" into the narrative of Palestinians as "sabre-rattling savages intent on destroying the Jews."

My mother eventually silenced this outspokenness and the threats disappeared. Several years later, I wrote the *Montreal Gazette* complaining about slanted Intifada coverage that ignored the concurrent Israeli bombing of Lebanon. That and a couple of articles about Palestine brought back the calls—insults, curses, breathtakingly violent threats.

Working at Palestine Hospital in Cairo in the early 1990s, a job that included West Bank and Gaza visits, I witnessed reprisals on a larger scale. Among many other incidents, I watched IDF soldiers chase a teenager through Jerusalem for waving a Palestinian flag. Bullets ricocheted off Old City walls, inches from my head. Days later, I visited the young man—he had escaped but lost an eye.

Back in Montreal, working for Medical Aid for Palestine meant constant vile threats and accusations. We developed thick skins, walked the thinnest lines, stayed careful. We never publicly acknowledged this constant reality: that Zionists harassed and threatened us with righteous impunity. Their fears as a community always protected, ours ignored.

The Ones Who Walk Away

I always felt that Ursula K. Le Guin's "The Ones Who Walk Away from Omelas" captures Israel-Palestine perfectly. The story describes the "abundantly pleasing" city of Omelas—whose utopia is sustained by one imprisoned child suffering in abject misery, a receptacle for all the foulness of the town. Some citizens don't care, others may have some initial trouble with the idea, but eventually the people of Omelas make peace with this necessary cruelty.

But every now and then, a citizen of Omelas "falls silent." Unable to endure this barbaric sacrifice, they "walk ahead into the darkness, and they do not come back." They never return, heading off to places "even less imaginable than the city of happiness."

A moral reckoning is coming. As Egyptian-Canadian author Omar El Akkad so eloquently put it, "One day, everyone will have always been against this." But a meaningful reckoning demands more than just our discomfort. We must examine and confront the institutions and systems that have enabled this moment.

The threats terrorizing my childhood, the decades of misinformation shaping Palestine discourse, the vociferous backlash against speaking out—these are all part of systematic efforts to maintain a narrative has justified the unjustifiable: the imminent and heartstoppingly brutal eradication of a people.

When Baraka Books publisher Robin Philpot and I conceived this anthology, I thought of Omelas. I wanted to reach out to those who walked away, who refused to trade others' misery for their contentment, who understood that the stories we hear are not always true, and that to confront harsh realities was an act of moral clarity.

People like Arfa Rana, Yara Jamal, Iman Kassam, who left or were forced out of good journalism jobs. Nora Loreto, Samira Mohyeddin—shut out of mainstream media. Libby Davies, Ehab Lotayef, Sean Tucker, Thoby King, Fred Hahn, Anna Zalik, the Jewish CEGEP teachers, all fighting to name the unmentionable. Yara Coussa, Hunaifa Malek, Sheima Benembarek, Safa Chebbi, and Duha Elmardi, putting their bodies on the line and suffering the consequences. Dr Yipeng Ge, Kathryn Grzejszczak, Health Workers Alliance, understanding that public safety, even globally, is public health. Elise Gravel, Kagiso Lesego Molope, Amy Blanding, amplifying the power of their voices. Gabor Maté, a balm and a beacon throughout the genocide.

I also wanted to recognize the Jewish community members speaking out across the country and the world. Even as their fierce courage tears apart family and community relationships, they shatter false equations of Judaism with Zionism, Jewish safety with Palestinian suffering, anti-genocide with antisemitism. Standing up against Zionist supremacy and ethnic cleansing has come at great personal sacrifice to each of them, and I see and honour that courage.

Between the River and the Sea

It was supposed to be "never again." But *never again* has eroded into a nostalgic musical refrain—a background melody that soothes our guilt, papers over cowardice, and invents a future. Now, those who were humming it have stopped, taking away what little comfort it provided.

Because Gaza is today. It is *now*. "Never again" demands that we recoil from this frenzy of death and withdraw our support—moral, political, economic—from the sadistic machinery of destruction and all who enable it.

If we do not, who are we? Who are we when we don't choose solidarity over comfort, truth-telling over silence, courage over complicity, justice over expediency? And what does this say about our governments, our media, our educational and cultural institutions? What does it reveal about our corporations, our financial systems, our communities, friends and families?

We have seen enough. The choices we make now define not only our politics, but our humanity. Yet we must choose, again and again, bravely, until justice becomes a lived reality for all people between each river and every sea.

Notes

1. "Gaza: Israeli army expands its use of quadcopters to kill more Palestinian civilians," Euromedmonitor.org, 4 June 2024.
2. Zeina Jamaluddine, et al, "Traumatic injury mortality in the Gaza Strip from Oct 7, 2023, to June 30, 2024: a capture–recapture analysis," *The Lancet*, Volume 405, Issue, 10477, 8 February 2025.
3. Tom McArthur, "Israeli settlement plans will 'bury' idea of a Palestinian state, minister says," BBC News, 14 August 2025.

PART ONE

ON THE FRONT LINES

CHAPTER 1

Desperately Seeking a Higher Moral Ground

Libby Davies

The times we are in. Like others, I wake up many a day with a sense of despair and chaos. Governments, including Canada, who fail to act as we witness genocide in Gaza. Hatred overtly stoked by a fascist US president. Deepening inequality layered on a climate emergency. As I move through the day, I remind myself over and over that there is growing global resistance seeking a higher moral ground. We strive for humanity to arrive at a better place.

On October 7, 2023, we learned of a shocking attack and the death of 1,200 Israelis, many of whom were attending a music festival, and the taking of hostages by Hamas. The immediate condemnation by the global community was swift and powerful. But what does it say about those same powerful forces that they remained largely silent when the disproportionate and vengeful bombardment by Israel, under the cover of "the right to defend" became a genocide of Palestinians?

The genocide itself and the resulting silence and failure of most governments to act in opposition to it, has horrified the world and galvanized people from all walks of life, both Palestinian and non-Palestinian, to take action. It has compelled us to speak out and demand a halt to the slaughter of tens of thousands of civilians—mothers and fathers, children, teenagers and students, journalists, emergency responders, doctors and nurses, teachers and elders—in civilian environments of home, school, emergency shelters, escape routes, and hospitals.

The global movement to stop the genocide has been impactful, resulting in a growing consciousness of the historical roots of the illegal displacement of Palestinians and occupation of Palestinian land. The global movement has also come at a cost for people speaking out. We have witnessed the heavy hand of Canadian institutions who have fired people, blacklisted others, torn down encampments, sent in the police, and censored accurate media reporting—because public opposition to the genocide and Canada's lack of action have been deemed hateful or even violent.

Unfortunately, the cost of speaking out is not new. In recent times, for example, during the Cold War, the civil rights movement, McCarthyism, the Vietnam war, and the Indigenous rights movement, people paid a heavy price for speaking out and taking action. I know from my own experience as a Canadian member of parliament for 18 years beginning in 1997, the ups and downs and costs of speaking out. I know the impact it can have personally and professionally.

I remember speaking out in Parliament about the importance of the Goldstone Report, based on a UN fact-finding mission into the Israeli assault on Gaza 2008-09. The attacks in Parliament by Conservative MPs were reminiscent of McCarthyism in the 1950s. In 2010, there were calls for me to resign my position as House Leader and Deputy Leader of the NDP, from Prime Minister Stephen Harper, MP Marc Garneau, Liberal foreign affairs critic Bob Rae, and others. This because I attended a rally in Vancouver, where my comments about the 1948 Nakba (in response to an unknown YouTuber who questioned me) were weaponized as antisemitic and a call to dismantle the state of Israel. Adding to the attack against me were comments in the media from Thomas Mulcair, also a deputy leader of the NDP. The unrelenting attempts to equate criticism of the state of Israel with calls to dismantle the state and antisemitism are a deliberate strategy to silence activists.

There were other occasions too, when speaking out in an environment of political censure came at a political and personal cost. Being at odds with the prevailing views of your colleagues can be uncomfortable and unnerving. Standing your ground is not always easy, especially when it creates conflict in your workplace or place of learning. Why is it so hard?

The answer is not hard to find. The influence of a Zionist narrative that deliberately couches criticism of Israel and its policies of apartheid as antisemitism; the broad adoption of the International Holocaust Remembrance Alliance (IHRA) definition of antisemitism—itself a campaign built on political threats of being branded as hateful and antisemitic—are powerful tools designed to silence people. As a result, self-censorship becomes a viable option for some individuals and organizations in order to protect themselves from electoral defeat, or being fired from a job, or even being charged with a crime. Some might be tempted to cast judgement on those faced with this dilemma of speaking out versus remaining silent. I believe it's better to focus on the roots of the fear and why it exists, rather than judge those who are victims of it.

Even though we may at times feel powerless or limited in our capacity to speak out, whether in elected office, in a work environment or in the community, I am convinced that the growing awareness and solidarity for overcoming all forms of hate, including antisemitism, Islamophobia, anti-Palestinian racism, denial of the impacts of colonization, or homophobia and transphobia, are more powerful than the forces who want to prevent the truth from being told. In this regard I have optimism, not fear, for the future.

While the consequences of speaking out are real, let us keep in front of us the courage of those who do speak out, and those who never gave up believing that documenting truth is essential and ongoing. I think here of someone like Robert Fisk, who spoke truth to power his whole life as a journalist. He and many others paved the way for a historical reckoning that cannot be dismissed in his coverage of the Middle East. His last book, published posthumously in 2024, *Night of Power: The Betrayal of the Middle East*, is a meticulous history of this issue.

Razing Palestine: Punishing Solidarity and Dissent in Canada is an essential addition to the public record and history. Too often, our experiences and struggles in movements for liberation and to overcome oppression and injustice are cast to the shadows or, worse, they are sabotaged by recorders of history who stake out a dominant narrative that upholds the oppressors. So let us share the experiences of speaking out. Let us not lose momentum: when we do speak up it brings about transformative change that we can be a part of, with confidence, pride and strength.

Photo: William Wilson

CHAPTER 2

"This Is What Happens When You Protest"

Yara Coussa

It was a late November night and Montreal was hosting a NATO summit of world leaders. Neither Palestine nor Gaza were on the agenda. It was a disgrace that after over a year of genocide, some of the most powerful nations in the world still could not admit what was going on. This was an injustice that I and many in Montreal felt compelled to speak against. That's why I joined several thousand people protesting the war, genocide, and oppression enabled by NATO states. I was there with a couple of friends unaffiliated with any group that was organizing. Unlike in past demonstrations where I joined various organizations, that day I felt that my body, and my body alone, was my tool for resistance.

The day of the protest dawned with a mix of anticipation and anxiety. I knew from past experiences that demonstrations like this might attract heightened police attention, but I was determined to make my voice heard. At the time I felt a sense of safety in the fact that I had no plans to stand out from the crowd or participate in any group that might be a target of the police. I was just a person with my friends speaking up about what we thought was right and wrong.

At 5:30 pm, I arrived at the demonstration equipped with my protest attire: a keffiyeh, plain clothes, and a medical mask. I carried goggles that a Palestinian medic gave me, just in case we were tear-gassed. Sadly, carrying around different kinds of protection is now seen as a necessary routine for any protester. Someone entrusted me with a banner bearing the word "Intifada." Holding the banner gave me a brief moment of strength and a pause from the overwhelming feeling of powerlessness that defined the night. While at first, the atmosphere was one of solidarity and purpose, as was common at protests for Palestine, anxiety crept in as riot police began gathering at the periphery. As we marched, the police trailed and flanked us. Their presence was, at least at first, a silent threat.

But the precarious peace wasn't meant to last and chaos erupted. Booms, paint bombs, pepper spray. The air thickened with tear gas as my vision blurred and my chest tightened. It was the worst-case reaction: I was seized by an asthma attack! I could barely breathe, let alone run. Through tears and gasps, I told my friends I had to leave. They held me and we began walking away. The rest of the protest was escaping faster past us. I worried that I was slowing everyone down, which caused me to spiral. *Why is my body so weak that it could not handle running like the rest?* I began slipping in and out of consciousness.

Finally, we were able to leave the protest and head down a side street off Viger. My friends told me we should keep walking. Expecting me to follow, they walked ahead. Everyone in that moment was focused on just getting themselves away from the violence. I wanted to do the same, but dizzy and weak, I took a second to gather myself. Desperate for air, I ripped off my keffiyeh.

Alone and weakened by tear gas, that's when they attacked me. Two police officers in riot gear shoved my face into a metal fence and demanded that I leave. Another stood by to oversee the assault. They kept shoving me, each time rougher than the last. I begged them to stop. My friends ran back when they heard the shouting and the clanging of my head against the metal. One friend yelled that I couldn't breathe. "Not breathing isn't going to stop you from walking," an officer yelled back.

The cops widened their circle and began beating my friends as well, pushing them to the ground, raining blows of their batons down upon all of us. My already barely functioning lungs started shutting down. It was evident that they had targeted the slowest protesters, the easiest ones to catch and hold down. We weren't fighting back; in fact, we were begging them to stop. Every time we attempted to get back up, they would trip us with their batons and send us back to the ground. They seemed to enjoy beating us. It couldn't have been clearer: Their intention was to humiliate and overpower us. We weren't a threat to them at all. I cried out, begging for their humanity, their mercy. "This is what happens when you protest," an officer sneered.

There was something methodical and creative in how they beat us. They used their batons, their shields, they hit my face, my head, my chest, my pubis, my legs. How was I supposed to leave if they kept hitting my legs? At one point I found myself making peace with the possibility that they would pull out their guns and just shoot us. I grieved my life. I thought of my mother and was so sorry for her. Would she think that I was a violent protester? Is that what they'd tell her? Would this be how I would be remembered in the eyes of my loved ones?

After what felt like an eternity the beating stopped as abruptly as it started. The police simply disappeared. We hurried away up other streets and were yelled at by supporters of Israel along the way. We found an alley where we could change our clothes and shed any visible marker that would attract police attention and more brutality. Then we went to the hospital, battered and blue. One of my friends needed surgery because her hand had been smashed when she tried to protect me from a baton. Even with her sacrifice I still was diagnosed with a concussion.

I now see the police as threatening entities, devoid of empathy. They beat me at the same time as Israel was bombing Lebanon. The police are monstrous, fueled by a thirst for control and oppression. Or am I describing Israel? It's all connected—the police, Israel, capitalism—systems that thrive on inflicting pain. Systems that demand you comply and then beat you down anyway. It feels like the end of the world, a dangerous moment where even the basic right to dissent is met with violence.

This violence has left its mark on me. I walk around with physical and emotional scars. Nightmares plague my sleep, dizziness and headaches disrupt my days, and the effects of the concussion are a constant reminder of the brutality. Even basic tasks like reading or following a conversation are difficult. I'm left feeling fragile, vulnerable, and deeply disillusioned. What's next? Am I meant to stop protesting for my country, for freedom, for life in order for me to be safe? Doesn't that mean that they've won?

I know their goal. They want us to stop protesting, to be obedient, to subjugate ourselves to their police state.

If they believe this will work, then they have underestimated our humanity and our determination to fight, because we will not give up. On the contrary, they have reinvigorated my anger, my rage, and the rage of my fellow protesters. I will never stop fighting back. They may have tried to break me, but I'll be damned if I let their attempt be successful.

Unbeknownst to both me and the police during my attack, a journalist took pictures of their violence. Today I am using these pictures to sue the police of Montreal. I am suing them for police brutality, for the over-policing of Palestinian protests, and for anti-Palestinian racism. My keffiyeh and my body made me a target. They made them see me as a terrorist and enemy. I'm not a terrorist. I will keep wearing my keffiyeh.

Fuck the police and long live the revolution. The following notes were taken from the Originating Application for Damages, filed against the Service de Police de la Ville de Montréal (SPVM) and the city of Montreal on January 9, 2025, in the Superior Court of Quebec.

Some modifications have been made for linguistic reasons, and names have been changed or masked to protect plaintiffs' privacy.

Plaintiff notes

1. At 6:45 pm, Police Officer name unknown, badge number 5461 ("Officer A") hits Plaintiff KP across the back of her head with his riot baton, taking her by surprise and causing her head to ring;
2. Police Officer name unknown, badge number 7854 ("Officer B") pushes Plaintiff Coussa against the wall, causing their head to ring;

3. Plaintiff Prentice tries to put herself between the officers and Plaintiff Coussa with her hands up to protect her head and face, as set forth in Exhibits P-8 to P-2514;
4. Officer A and Officer B, aided by a third police officer, surround Plaintiffs Prentice and Coussa and corner them against the fence, as set forth in Exhibits P-8 to P-25;
5. Officer A hits Plaintiff Prentice repeatedly in the arms and hands, breaking her right pinkie; Officer A and Officer B throw Plaintiff Prentice to the ground, as set forth in Exhibit P-10 to P-25;
6. Another demonstrator, JD takes Plaintiff Coussa by the arm and tries to lead them away from the police;
7. Officer A and Officer B attack the Plaintiffs KP, Coussa, and AB with their batons and shields, making it difficult for any of them to walk;
8. Throughout the assault, Plaintiff Coussa begs and cries for the police officers to stop;
9. Officer A and Officer B hit Plaintiff Coussa on the thorax, breast, back, pubis, butt, stomach, tooth, and face; Plaintiff Coussa is afraid the assault will hospitalize them or that they might die;
10. Officer A and Officer B scream and shout at Plaintiffs KP, Coussa, and AB telling them to move north-west along Rue St-Alexandre;
11. JD tries to pull Plaintiff Coussa away from the attacking police officers and into an alley;
12. They tell the police that they are trying to leave, but the police officers hit them with their batons to keep them along the same path;
13. Plaintiffs KP, Coussa, and AB walk northwest along Rue St-Alexandre as Officer A and Officer B continue to attack them with their batons and shields;
14. As Plaintiffs KP, Coussa, and AB walk as directed, Officer A and Officer B throw each one to the ground in turn;

15. Officer A and Officer B continue to attack Plaintiffs KP, Coussa, and AB with their shields and batons as they are on the ground and as they try to help each other up;
16. Officer A kicks Plaintiff KP's legs out from under her as soon as she stands up, again knocking her to the ground;
17. Officer A continues to hit Plaintiff KP as she is on the ground, and as she stands back up;
18. Officer A and Officer B scream at Plaintiffs KP, Coussa, and AB "Move!", "Bouge!" etc. and shove and hit them as they continue to move in the direction indicated, having never stopped except when knocked to the ground;
19. Officer A screams at Plaintiff KP to stop looking him in the eyes, then jabs her in the stomach with a riot baton, knocking the wind out of her and knocking her to the ground;
20. The third police officer appears to tell Officer A that his actions are out of line;
21. A dozen or so police officers are in the middle of Rue St-Alexandre watching Plaintiffs KP, Coussa, and AB get assaulted;
22. The experience is thoroughly terrifying and humiliating;
23. Officer A and Officer B yell at Plaintiffs KP, Coussa, and AB to move;
24. Plaintiff AB is knocked to the ground, and upon standing up, is immediately pushed down again;
25. The Plaintiffs tell the police officers that they are moving, but that Plaintiff Coussa is having an asthma attack and can't breathe ("J'arrive pas a respirer");
26. Officer A and Officer B tell Plaintiff Coussa that not breathing does not prevent you from walking;
27. Police Officers do not offer or assist with decontamination;
28. Plaintiff Coussa asks Officer A and Officer B where their humanity is ("Où est votre humanité?");
29. One of Officer A or Officer B tells Plaintiff Coussa that this is what happens when you go to a demonstration ("C'est ça qui se passe quand tu vas manifester");

30. Officer A and Officer B continue to attack Plaintiffs Prentice, Coussa, and AB with batons and shields as they continue to walk in the direction Officer A and Officer B want; Officer A and Officer B yell to go faster, and express frustration that they are losing the crowd;
31. As Plaintiffs KP, Coussa, and AB arrive at Boulevard René-Lévesque, within sight of the pedestrians and cars travelling along that road, Officer A and Officer B stop attacking and let them cross;
32. Plaintiffs KP, Coussa, and AB were continuously attacked as they walked along Rue St-Alexandre from Rue de la Gauchetière Ouest to Boulevard René-Lévesque, a distance of about 200 metres;
33. Only once Plaintiffs KP, Coussa, and AB are within sight of passersby traveling along Boulevard René-Lévesque do Officer A and Officer B stop attacking them.

Aftermath notes

1. On 22 November at 7 pm, after the excessive use of force by police officers, Plaintiff Coussa has crossed Boulevard René-Lévesque and begins to take stock of their injuries:
   a. They have difficulty breathing and pain in their chest;
   b. They have gaps in their memory;
   c. They have pain in their left chest, left shoulder blade, left buttock, left shin, mons pubis, and stomach;
   d. They experience pale, cold, and clammy skin; shallow, rapid, and difficult breathing; acute anxiety; rapid and irregular heartbeat; and dry mouth;
2. At 8 pm, a medic provides Plaintiff Coussa with an asthma pump, which does little to ease their symptoms;
3. At 9 pm, they are triaged at Jean-Talon Hospital; the nurse suspects they had an asthma crisis and have a concussion;
4. Plaintiff Coussa is reassessed by the triaging nurse many times as they become increasingly nauseous and sensitive to light and sound;

5. At 11:30 pm, Plaintiff Coussa is moved to a different waiting room to ease their concussion symptoms;
6. At 10 am the next morning, Plaintiff Coussa is seen by a doctor and is given an ultrasound, a brain scan, and a thorax scan; Plaintiff Coussa is diagnosed with a concussion and ordered to bed rest for a week, as set forth in Exhibit P-64;
7. Their concussion symptoms make them unable to attend to daily domestic tasks such as cooking, cleaning, or washing dishes;
8. Over the next two months Plaintiff Coussa has persistent difficulty breathing and a return of asthma symptoms which had not affected them since childhood;
9. Plaintiff Coussa develops dark and painful bruises on their left chest, left shoulder blade, left buttock, left shin, mons pubis, and stomach, as set forth in Exhibits P-65 to P-72;
10. Their bruises fill them with a renewed sense of disgust and violation whenever they see them, leading to an ongoing loss of sex drive and difficulty with intimacy that is greatly damaging to their sense of self;
11. Their feelings of incapacitation, despair, and depression damage their self-esteem and stain their friendships and romantic relationships;
12. In the months following, Plaintiff Coussa experiences difficulty sleeping, hypervigilance, panic attacks, flashbacks, prolonged stress and anxiety, and fear of police officers;
13. They have recurring nightmares about seeing Plaintiff Prentice and JD on the ground while they scream "Stop! Stop! S'il vous plaît arrêtez! Please stop!";
14. On 24 November, they are unable to follow conversations or stay awake for prolonged amounts of time without extreme headaches; they have difficulty staying alert and focused, leading to cooking fires and lost possessions;
15. From 25 November, Plaintiff Coussa is on work leave without pay: they have yet to return to work, as set forth in Exhibit P-73;

16. Plaintiff Coussa has nightmares, constant dizziness, constant headaches, and constant nausea, and needs to wear sunglasses at all times because light worsens their headache; the bruising covering their whole body prevents them from sleeping properly;
17. Plaintiff Coussa is unable to engage in their wellness practices of reading, writing, painting, or high-intensity workouts;
18. 1 December, they are examined by Dr Saiden Khadir at ELNA Médical - Metro Medic Centre-Ville and diagnosed with PTSD, as set forth in Exhibit P-74;
19. Plaintiff Coussa's premenstrual syndrome is exceptionally characterized by nausea, vomiting, and abdominal pain that cannot be managed by over-the-counter pain medication, as set forth in Exhibit P-75;
20. On 7 December, Plaintiff Coussa starts their menstruation two weeks late; the pain continues and is unusually extreme;
21. On 20 December, Plaintiff Coussa has a follow-up appointment with Dr Khadir, where she finds that their concussion, short-term memory, psychological distress, and asthma symptoms have worsened; Dr Khadir refers them to a neurologist, as set forth in Exhibit P-75;
22. On 21 December, Plaintiff Coussa experiences consistent and extreme nausea with regular vomiting, unable to hold down food or liquids which causes them to suffer from dehydration; symptoms last into the following week;
23. On 24 December, Plaintiff Coussa is triaged at the Jewish General Hospital emergency room, given an intravenous drip, and treated with cortisol before being discharged late that night pending a follow-up appointment with a neurologist;
24. They are forced to spend Christmas eve, a sacred holiday for their family who had flown in from Lebanon, in the hospital and could not celebrate with them;

25. The cortisol makes their heart race uncomfortably fast, and makes them feel like they're dying; their only recourse from the anxiety is scalding hot showers;
26. On 29 December, Plaintiff Coussa is examined by neurologist Dr Daniel Shedid at the Centre hospitalier de l'Université de Montréal; it is determined they will need further follow-up.

Photo: Hunaifa Malik

CHAPTER 3

Our Solidarity Is Not a Crime: Surveillance, Protest, and the Politics of Being Seen

Hunaifa Malik

I feel just as nervous as last week. I am concerned that there will be counter-protesters, media, and an intimidating police presence given the tensions in Montreal following the recent "vandalization" of several McGill buildings by BDS supporters, and the plan to march down to the US Consulate. I have a knot in my stomach all day and think hard about how to dress to best blend in with the crowd.

I head out at 2 pm beneath yet another overcast sky; it is as if the heavy clouds are commiserating with the protesters. Arriving at the nearest metro station around 2:30 pm, I follow a man draped in a Palestinian flag to the protest site. The crowd has gathered across the four-point intersection surrounding the American consulate, in the heart of downtown Montreal. Signs are written in Arabic, English, and French, and speakers blare revolutionary music in the background, including the now-familiar tune "Libre Palestina."

Police scatter throughout, their highlighter-yellow vests indistinguishable from those of the organizers, who distribute hand warmers and Palestinian flags. A large sign with a scratched barcode stands out: "1948-2025 — Gaza is not and never has been for sale." Two Orthodox Jewish men stand solemnly, their signs proclaiming that Judaism and the Torah reject Zionism and the Israeli state. Shoppers and traffic continue around the protest, with some cars honking in support and pedestrians pausing briefly to watch before continuing on with their day. Two merch tables on St. Catherine Street sell keffiyehs, flags, stickers, and the like. Unlike the previous protest, this crowd seems generally older, with fewer young people or families present.

Protesters and event organizers exchange nods and embraces, greeting one another in a blend of Arabic, English, and French. Many hold signs depicting maps of Palestine in the colours of the Palestinian flag. Multiple people shoot photos and videos on raised phones while several organizers wield video cameras throughout the crowd. As time passes, the crowd continues to build and sing along to the music continuing in the background. Visibility appears to be a key goal; several demonstrators wave massive Palestinian, Lebanese, and Syrian flags into the street for passersby to see. Organizers circulate with donation bins for Hands for Charity, collecting donations for Gazans. Many protesters, organizers, and even some police officers keep their faces covered. While the racial composition of the protesters is diverse (multiple variations in skin colour, religious garments, languages), the police presence is strikingly homogenous—almost entirely white.

Eventually, the music fades and a speaker addresses the growing crowd with a series of chants in all three languages that many seem already well versed in. "Donald Trump you will see, Palestine will be free," "Free, free Palestine," "Libre Palestina," "Donald Trump casse-toi, Palestine n'est pas à toi." Drums and a trumpet accompany the rhythmic chants. The speaker's voice carries over the intersection: "Resistance is justified, the people are occupied!" Protesters respond in unison, "No justice, no peace!" and "We the people will not be silenced, liberation now!" The chants escalate and echo through the streets—"We will free our people, we will free our land, get the zions out out out!" "Zionism is fascism! Tout le monde déteste le zionisme!" As the crowd spills further into the street, cutting off traffic, police take a more active role, directing vehicles around the demonstration.

The speaker calls out Justin Trudeau: "The prime minister has said BDS has no place in Canada but calls for a boycott against the US." The crowd responds: "Shame!" The speaker's voice grows firm. "The history books will reveal who stood on what side, and our calls will continue to echo in the streets until Palestine is liberated from the river to the sea." The crowd responds with a deafening chant, "From the river to the sea, Palestine will be free!"—I watch an elderly man slam his walking stick into the snow with each chant. Another protester gets a keffiyeh from one of the merch tables and immediately drapes it over his shoulders. The mic passes from speaker to speaker, each reinforcing similar themes. One organizer speaks out to those who do not believe in the resistance. He insists they "learn the truth about the Palestinian people who have resisted since 1948. Palestine is not for sale. Al Aqsa is not for sale. Gaza is not for sale." He ended with a firm statement: "Our people are not defeatable. Our resistance is not erasable."

A native Palestinian speaker takes the mic next and frequently refers to the Palestinian people as "the ummah." He concludes with a call for "Takbir," to which the crowd roars back, "Allahu Akbar!" His voice cracks at several points and as he makes his final plea: "Inshallah, Allah will deliver us soon! Keep your imaan, keep your faith, be the voice for the people. We are the people of the resistance."

He passes the mic to a new face—a Ugandan ally wearing a resistance beret. He speaks of his own country's struggle, standing in solidarity with today's movement: "We are one people, one resistance." As the crowd breaks for the afternoon

Asr prayer around 3:40 pm, organizers lay down makeshift prayer mats of plastic tarp in the muddy streets of downtown Montreal. Muslim protesters line up shoulder to shoulder in prayer with their co-religionists. Afterward, the demonstration continues with a march through downtown along St. Catherine Street. A truck equipped with speakers blares resistance music, leading the way as police form a perimeter around the crowd. The march is slow but purposeful as light snow begins to fall around 4 pm. As I make my exit, the music and honking horns carry on, reverberating through the city and upward to my apartment.

Although there were many bystanders along the march, I did not see any counter-protesters or anyone from the media. The only direct interaction I witness occurs when an officer attempts to let a vehicle through an intersection as protesters walk through it. A woman quickly intervenes: "Hey, you can't do that. We're allowed to walk here." The officer does not respond, but continues to wave the vehicle through with his whistle in his mouth. The car has priority.

This excerpt is from my field notes written after a series of pro-Palestine protests in Montreal between February and April 2025. My goal was to explore how evidence is constructed in protest spaces, including how protesters use speech, symbols, and performance to assert legitimacy, document injustice, and mobilize support. I was interested in the epistemologies of protest: how knowledge is made, shared, and contested in the streets. But the field had other plans. What emerged was a far more complex social terrain.

Surveillance, racialized policing, spiritual resistance, intergenerational solidarity, and the emotional labour of protest all surfaced as central dynamics. I found myself documenting not only how evidence was constructed but also how it was constrained. The project became as much about what could not be said as about what was. In this way, the protests revealed themselves not just as sites of evidence-making, but as microcosms of broader political tensions between freedom and fear, solidarity and surveillance, and the right to protest and the reality of being policed. That winter, in spite of the barriers and costs associated with protest, tens of thousands across Canada protested weekly in support of Palestine. These protests functioned as counter-publics, where marginalized voices articulated alternative narratives of justice, often in defiance of dominant discourses and institutional silencing.

Across the several protests I attended in Montreal, one pattern remained consistent: the homogeneity of the police. While the crowd reflected a visibly diverse mix of races, faiths, genders, and ages, the police presence —white, male, in their 30s—was a sharp contrast. This visual dissonance was not lost on protesters, but was a silent but potent reminder of who is empowered to watch and who is watched.

Although police rarely intervened directly, their presence shaped the atmosphere. Amongst those of us who were not only protesting but publicly associated with the movement (assumed through our visible racial and religious identities), the police presence was on the forefront, resulting in a shared sense of fear and unease. I carried a knot in my stomach throughout this fieldwork. It settled there quietly, sometimes flaring into full-body tension, sometimes dulling into background noise. But it never left. It was there as I approached the US Consulate, as I scanned the crowd for counter-protesters, as I stood near police officers whose expressions I could not read. I was never quite certain if the police were there for us or *for* us. This ambiguity haunted every protest. Although the officers stood still, often silent, their presence was never neutral. Their uniforms, their expressions, their whiteness, all signaled power. And I, as a visibly Muslim woman, was acutely aware of how easily that power could shift. I was not just observing surveillance; I was subject to it.

Surveillance was a choreographed performance of power and control. The stillness of the police, their unreadable expressions, and the calculated distance they maintained were calibrated to remind us that we were monitored, recorded, and potentially punishable. The performance of surveillance was itself a form of discipline. We were meant to feel the unspoken threat of what could follow.

It was not hard to imagine our images being fed into databases, our chants flagged as threats, and our identities noted. And these fears were not hypothetical. Students have been investigated, employees suspended, organizers quietly blacklisted. In this way, surveillance was a pipeline. A silent scan today could mean a disciplinary email tomorrow. We did not need to be arrested to feel punished. We only needed to be seen.

The fear I felt is not unique to me. It is shared by many who protest, especially those who are racialized or otherwise marked as "other." And it is a reminder that the right to protest is not equally distributed, but is shaped by who you are, how you look, and what you are protesting.

And yet, there we were, week after week, standing across the street from the police, armed only with our flags. For many of us, there was no other avenue for expressing our grief, our rage, and our resistance—not only against the occupation, but against our own country's complicity in the genocide unfolding in Gaza.

These protests reveal the conditional nature of political rights in Canada—how freedom of expression, assembly, and dissent are not guaranteed equally, but are negotiated through the lenses of race, religion, and political alignment. Protest is not just a political act but a diagnostic tool that reveals the health of a democracy, not by how it treats the powerful but by how it responds to the marginalized. These protests are not only acts of activism and resistance in the face of surveillance and alienation, they are warnings about the fragility of political rights and the elasticity of state tolerance in Canada.

At one protest, a speaker said, "Our flags are not weapons, and our solidarity is not a crime—it is humanity." The power of that statement reverberated through the crowd and echoed with a chorus of chants. It landed with particular weight given the growing criminalization of pro-Palestinian solidarity in Canada and elsewhere. Everyone there knew someone who had been targeted—fired from a job, investigated by their university, harassed online, or quietly alienated from their community—simply for expressing support for Palestine. The line between political expression and punishment felt increasingly thin. In that moment, the words were a reminder that in the current political climate, even holding a flag could be construed as a threat.

At multiple protests in Montreal, participants spoke openly of raids, harassment, and political intimidation. These were not abstract fears but lived experiences, shared through megaphones and murmured in side conversations. Protesters were acutely aware of how their actions might be misframed by media, political actors, and police. Several speeches referenced the lack of media coverage or the distortion of their message. One protest organizer that I spoke to noted, "The media only came at the start of the protests around October 7 to try to use it against us. They don't want the truth to spread."

For many, the act of being seen by police, media, or simply passersby, was itself a form of vulnerability. To be visible in a protest space, especially while racialized, was to risk being surveilled, misrepresented, and targeted. That gaze was not neutral; it was layered with suspicion, power, and the threat of consequence.

And yet, visibility was also a form of resistance as a refusal to disappear. In response to their exclusion from mainstream public discourse, protesters made *their* discourses public. They took to the streets not only to be seen and heard, but to reclaim the authority to name their truths, mourn their dead, and envision a future for Palestine. With chants echoing across intersections, flags raised high, and phones documenting every moment, the protest space became a platform—an embodied, collective intervention in a public sphere that had otherwise rendered them invisible or illegible. In the absence of institutional recognition of any sort, the street became the stage, the archive, and the amplifier. And there, on the streets, protesters went well beyond political dissent. Using statistics, symbols, emotions, and spiritual expression, they made the public square into a classroom, a sanctuary, a battleground, and a home, often all at once.

In a political climate where pro-Palestinian activism is increasingly criminalized, the decision to be physically present, filmed, or named was not taken lightly. Protesters knew they were being watched. They knew that their images might circulate beyond the crowd, that their words might be taken out of context, that their presence might be used against them. And still, they came. In this way, protest became both an act of expression and an act of defiance. It was a refusal to be silenced by fear and a refusal to allow the threat of surveillance to dictate the boundaries of political speech. Protesters made themselves visible not because it was safe, but because it was necessary.

In this way, the protests are not only acts of resistance but reclamation that expand our understanding of how people make truth together, particularly when traditional institutions render them illegible. This use of protest has broader implications for how we conceptualize political voice and agency: not as making policy claims intelligible to the state but as claiming space, time, and meaning within a broader public—whether or not the state listens.

The protests I attended in Montreal and the broader "pro-Palestine" movement in Canada is not just about Palestine. The way these protests are portrayed by the state, media, and society signals who gets to speak, who gets to be seen, and who is allowed to belong. But beyond showing us where we stand today, these protests showcase powerful counter-publics, creating spaces where grief is not hidden and where political speech is not reserved for the powerful.

CHAPTER 4

Policing the Window: The Case of the Indigo 11

Thoby King

Photo: CP24/YouTube

In the wee hours of November 10, 2023, a group of activists stuck posters and splashed red paint onto the storefront window of an Indigo bookstore in downtown Toronto. The posters featured a full-page headshot of the company's founder and CEO Heather Reisman under the heading "Funding Genocide" and called her the "Chief Occupation Lover." It was all done up in Indigo's house style complete with the brand's signature "Heather's Pick" logo. By then, a month since the October 7 attacks, Israel's military had killed approximately 11,000 people in Gaza, mostly women and children. This, of course, was only the beginning.

The postering was part of a long-running effort[1] to hold Reisman and her company to account for their support for Israel and its military, particularly through the HESEG Foundation,[2] which Reisman founded with husband Gerald Schwartz in 2005 to provide scholarships for Israeli Defence Force soldiers without family in Israel. Direct actions like this for Palestine had erupted around the world as people fought back against the Israeli onslaught and its defenders. That same morning, coordinated actions[3] in Toronto, Hamilton, Montreal, and Ottawa shut down plants that manufactured weapons parts used by the IDF. Those actions, involving hundreds of activists from multiple organizations across the four cities, were almost entirely ignored by local media.

The Indigo case was a different story.

At around 5:00 am, an Indigo employee discovered the posters and called 911. Court documents revealed[4] months later that Reisman herself contacted Toronto police chief Myron Demkiw that day, speaking to him twice during the course of the investigation. The content of those conversations remains unknown.

Photos of the poster-stricken window quickly made their way online, the angry red globs and hurried paste-up incongruous against the pristine storefront. As Indigo staff cleaned off the window, the usual pundits and lobbyists took to the internet to exclaim their horror. "Kristallnacht has come to Toronto," pronounced the *Toronto Sun*'s Joe Warmington, referring to the Nazi pogrom that then had its anniversary.[5]

Michael Levitt, president and CEO of the pro-Israel Friends of Simon Wiesenthal Center (FSWC), released a statement calling the postering a "vile antisemitic attack," a line that became the headline at both CTV and CP24 before the morning was over.[6] Initial coverage emphasized Reisman's Jewish heritage, taking as given that this was the reason for the posters, and made no mention of HESEG or what the accusation of funding genocide might have been about.[7]

Then came the arrests.

On November 14, three Toronto Police officers grabbed Nisha Toomey, an educator with a PhD in social justice education, in a parking lot. She later described being "bombarded by three officers," her car seized, home searched, and devices taken while she was held for nearly 10 hours.[8] Police found their next targets in a Signal group chat on Toomey's phone.[9] Eight days later, they arrested 10 more people during a series of brutal pre-dawn raids, all quite extraordinary for a crime of postering and more typical of a gun or drug bust, as a legal expert later observed.[10]

Among the people arrested that morning was York University professor Lesley Wood, herself proudly Jewish. "At 5:30 am, seven police officers broke down the door of our home and dragged my partner and I out of bed," she wrote in a statement released the following week. "We were handcuffed and our house was searched. What were they looking for? They ignored the menorah. They ignored the song sheet from Jews Against Genocide lying on the kitchen table. Instead, they took us to the station and charged us."[11] In another of that morning's raids, police broke a door down only to discover that they had the wrong address. That afternoon, as the accused sat in police custody, protesters gathered outside a Toronto police station to show support and call for their release.[12]

The next day, Toronto police launched an aggressive public relations offensive. The chief, attending a Police Board meeting that morning, discussed the city's "staggering" rise in hate incident reports and promised to "aggressively uncover and pursue any suspected incidents of hate-motivated behaviour."[13] He made sure to mention that the cost of all this would be "significant." His address was followed hours later by a press release, naming the members of the group that the press dubbed the "Indigo 11," situating them firmly in the hate crime narrative.[14] Among the accused were an immigration consultant, a schoolteacher, and multiple academics.

All eleven were charged with mischief over $5,000 and conspiracy to commit an indictable offence. The postering, the statement announced, was "being treated as a suspected hate-motivated offence" in a "hate-motivated Mischief Over $5000 investigation" by the Hate Crime Unit. Meanwhile, a spokesperson was deployed to declare to the media, without qualification, "the victim was specifically targeted because they are [or are perceived to be] Jewish."[15] The accused's names and pictures were published widely, often framed as perpetrators of "vile antisemitic vandalism."[16]

On November 30, a group of activists led by the Jews Say No to Genocide Coalition mounted another solidarity demonstration outside the Indigo where it all started. Each brought a copy of the offending poster, which they hoped to tape up on the same window in a re-enactment of the so-called crime. When a row of security guards made this impossible, the demonstrators held the posters in the air. Speakers included Dr. Wood and author Naomi Klein, who called on police to drop the charges.[17] Instead, the cops laid the additional charge of harassment against all

11 accused, again describing the charges in a press release peppered with references to a "suspected" hate motive. All told, the word "hate" appears 26 times across the force's two press releases announcing the charges.

As the court proceedings began, the accused learned the scale of the police operation, which included over 70 officers. As one of the 11's legal team put it, "nighttime raids, no-knock entries, obtaining DNA from paintbrushes, (and) thousands of pages of disclosure—all for some paint and posters."

The framing of the posters as a hate crime, advanced by the police with the help of pro-Israel groups like FSWC and the Centre for Israeli and Jewish Affairs (CIJA)[18] and embraced by credulous reporters, did much to obscure both the legal and factual realities of the Indigo case.

The phrase "hate crime" does not actually exist in Canadian law. Canada's Criminal Code does not include the phrase, but does set out a handful of hate-related offences, namely advocating genocide, public incitement of hatred, willful promotion of hatred, and willful promotion of antisemitism. While the police hinted, in their two press releases on the Indigo case, that they were considering invoking these provisions, the charges never materialized. The Code also has a provision for mischief motivated by hate for an "identifiable group," including racial and religious minorities. However, that provision only applies to places "primarily used" by that group, such as places of worship and religious schools, not big box stores.

For any other crime, an alleged hate motive is not an element of the offence and does not form part of the charge.

Rather, hatred on the basis of race, religion, or similar grounds can be considered in sentencing, one of a laundry list of aggravating and mitigating factors that also includes things like the accused's employment status and the vulnerability of the victim. Importantly, though, these factors only become relevant *after* an accused person, presumed innocent, has been found guilty. If and when that happens, it is the Crown, not the police, that marshals the evidence to argue which factors call for a more serious sentence.

Put simply, the cops' official-sounding claim that this was an act of "hate-motivated mischief," featured so prominently in their press statements and echoed throughout the news reporting, had almost no legal significance. Rather than describing the charge, the hate claim was a free-standing aspersion, a smear dressed up in legal language and loudly broadcast to the public, unsupported by evidence. The cart was put before the horse then rolled over the accused's reputation. Here, the police ventured out of their legal role in investigating crime and laying charges, squarely into the realm of political theatre.

The actual charges laid were much more mundane than the coverage indicated. Mischief, a familiar charge for activists, refers to any act that willfully damages someone else's property or interferes with the lawful use of it, while the ominous-sounding conspiracy charge simply reflected the allegation that the accused had worked together on the alleged mischief. As to harassment, added several days after the others, this charge rested on the dubious allegation that the posters at the Yorkville Indigo caused Reisman to reasonably fear for her personal safety. Small wonder that, by November 2024, the Crown had withdrawn all 11 harassment charges. The remaining charges amounted to an allegation that the accused worked together to make a mess on the store window.

Predictably, the technical distinction between hate as an element of the charge and hate as a motive alleged by police caused some confusion in the media. *The Globe and Mail,* in a November 2023 piece, initially described the 11 as being charged "with hate-motivated mischief," then issued a correction clarifying that "[t]hey were charged with mischief and the Toronto police allege the offence was motivated by hate." [19] However, articles published months later by CBC[20] and the *National Post*[21] at the time of writing this article, still feature the very language that the *Globe* felt the need to correct, inaccurately referring to a charge of "hate-motivated mischief."

Clearly, for Toronto police, the legalities were secondary to the political project of framing Palestine solidarity as antisemitic and flexing their muscles in the face of the movement.

The raids, arrests, and public relations offensive were part of a massive expansion of policing under what the force called Project Resolute.[22] In the weeks after October 7 and the start of Israel's genocide, citing the "staggering"[23] spike in reported hate incidents in the city, police began pouring resources into their aggressive response. At the centre of the project was the Hate Crime Unit, quintupled in size in October 2023 from six officers to 32.

It was immediately apparent that the police had little interest in distinguishing between real acts of racist violence—people attacked with a bike chain at a masjid or bomb threats at Jewish schools—and non-violent acts in solidarity with Palestine.[24] The enlarged Hate Crime Unit was put in charge of the "investigation of any occurrence generated as a result of protests and/or demonstrations related to the Middle East conflict," whether or not there was any allegation of either hate or crime. This administrative maneuver made explicit the conflation of Palestine advocacy with antisemitism, officially linking the hate crime label to any act of civil disobedience for Palestine, such as the November 10 Indigo postering.

As op-eds denounced Palestine solidarity demonstrations as "Hamas-supporting 'hate fests,'"[25] the police showed a similar hostility. Week after week, phalanxes of riot cops attended peaceful marches, sealing off intersections deemed inappropriate for protest while the police drone buzzed overhead. Officers on horseback ploughed through crowds to disperse them. On multiple occasions, protesters were pepper sprayed, slammed on the pavement, and beaten into submission. A camera-topped van equipped with facial recognition software trailed marches, part of what one officer described as the Toronto Police Service's (TPS) "fully integrated intelligence-sharing model" in coordination with the Royal Canadian Mounted Police (RCMP) and Canadian Security Intelligence Service (CSIS).[26] Movement leaders were tracked down and arrested months after the fact for participating in sit-ins and other peaceful actions. Police solicited arrestees to turn informant. All of this came at great cost to the taxpayer, with CBC reporting $40 million in overspending for the city during 2024 as a result of Project Resolute. Other Canadian cities saw similar crackdowns on Palestine activists.

Meanwhile, Ontario's Ministry of the Attorney General, responsible for criminal prosecution, likewise showed an institutional animus to the Palestine movement. As some prosecutors contemplated withdrawing charges against activists, they faced pressure from inside the ministry not to let charges drop, or to seek harsher sanctions than they otherwise might. The pressure came from the ministry's Hate Crime Working Group, a "secretive committee" with a history of targeting Palestine activists[27] that counted among its members the Crown in charge of the Indigo case. The same ministry, in fall of 2023, blackballed applicants for placements, jobs, and clerkships from Toronto Metropolitan University's law school[28] for signing a letter demanding the school oppose Israel's actions in Gaza.[29]

Such were the institutions that aligned against the 11 people accused of postering the Indigo window. And while their case was likely the most publicized prosecution of Palestine activists in Canada, it was by no means unique, with one organization counting 105 arrests for Palestine activism from October 7, 2023 to February 2025 in Toronto alone. Tactics like those used against the 11—the pre-dawn raids, the surprise arrests, the hate smears, the grasping after dubious charges—all became recurring features of the state's efforts to suppress the movement through whatever means were available.

Take, for instance, the Calgary man charged with causing a disturbance, also in November 2023, reportedly for leading a chant of "From the river to the sea, Palestine will be free." There, too, police publicly alleged a hate motivation. That charge was stayed by the Crown less than two weeks later, the Crown likely seeing that it was legally and constitutionally problematic.

Or take the case of Yves Engler, the independent journalist charged in February 2025 with harassment for social media comments calling a Zionist internet personality a "fascist" and "genocide supporter."[30] When Engler wrote critically about the arrest on his website[31] and refused release terms that would prevent his doing so further, Montreal police laid another harassment charge, this time alleging that he was harassing *them* through his writing. The police then held Engler for five days before a court ordered him released on bail.

What these cases do not exemplify is a proportionate, dispassionate application of criminal law to the actions of the accused. To the contrary, they show the police reaching for ways of silencing those who might challenge the domestic political status quo around Israel. In this process, the police's role is not to enforce the law, not to bring the accused and evidence before the courts to determine what, if any, crimes have been committed. Rather, it is to curtail speech not approved of by the state through extrajudicial punishments by violence and humiliation. The law has very little to do with it.

The Indigo 11 remained a Canadian news story as the charges moved through Ontario's sluggish criminal process. The case even received some notice in the Middle East, including a *Times of Israel* blog post demanding that the accused be "taught a lesson that they and their admirers will never forget,"[32] and an op-ed in *Al Jazeera* by legal scholar Faisal Kutty calling for the charges to be dropped.[33] By October 2024, the Indigo 11 had their own Wikipedia article detailing the facts of the case and ensuing controversy.

Notes

1. Canadians for Justice and Peace in the Middle East (CJPME), Boycott Campaign: Indigo Books & Music Inc, CPMG.org.
2. HESEG Foundation, HESEG.com.
3. "200 Workers Block Access to Toronto Weapons-Maker L3Harris," World Beyond War, 10 November 2023.
4. "Indigo CEO Heather Reisman spoke directly to Toronto police chief hours after store was defaced by pro-Palestinian protesters: court documents," *Toronto Star*, 22 November 2025.
5. Joe Warmington, "Tolerance of racism against Jews has Toronto at turning point and police on hot seat," *Toronto Sun*, 10 November 2023.
6. "Latest Antisemitic Attack Targets Toronto Indigo Store and its Jewish CEO," Friends of Simon Wiesenthal Center, 10 November 2023.
7. Chris Fox, "'Vile antisemitic attack': Police investigating graffiti targeting Indigo CEO outside downtown Toronto store," *CTV News*, 10 November 2023.
8. Nisha Toomey, "I'm One of the Indigo 11. Here's Why I Did It," *The Maple*, 20 January 2025.
9. Ashleigh Stewart, "Dropped charges, police overreach: How the Indigo 11 case fell apart," *Global News*, 27 April 2025.
10. Martin Lukacs, "In stunning pre-dawn raids, Toronto police 'terrorize' Palestine activists," *The Breach*, 24 November 2023.
11. Lesley Wood, "Never Again for Anyone and Charges of Antisemitism," Lesleybikes.Wordpress.org, 20 November 2023.
12. "Arrests in vandalism at Indigo store sparking pro-Palestinian protest at Toronto police station," *Toronto Star*, 22 November 2023.
13. Toronto Police Services Board Meeting. Live Stream, YouTube. 23 November 2023.
14. "Arrests Made in Hate-Motivated Mischief Investigation, Bay Street and Bloor Street West area, Eleven arrests made," News Release, Toronto Police Service, 23 November 2023.
15. Mike Hager and Sean Fine. "Toronto police charge 11 in Indigo store vandalism, report spike in hate incidents," *The Globe and Mail*, 23 November 2023.
16. "In the Bad Books," *Toronto Sun*, X, 23 November 2023.
17. Naomi Klein and Emma Paling, "Naomi Klein to Heather Reisman: Charges must be dropped against Indigo 11," *The Breach*, 30 November 2023.
18. "We're grateful here in Toronto to see that our police are giving the signal that we all have a right to our opinion, we all have a right to demonstrate, we all have a right to take a political position. But we don't

have a right to vandalize people's property and to terrify people based on their race or social background." CIJA tweet on X, 8 January 2024.
19. Mike Hager and Sean Fine, "Toronto police charge 11 in Indigo store vandalism, report spike in hate incidents," *The Globe and Mail*, 23 November 2023.
20. Jane Gerster, "Crown drops charges against 4 accused in Indigo bookstore vandalism," *CBC News*, 22 May 2024.
21. "The odious smear campaign against Heather Reisman and Indigo books," NP Comment, *National Post*, 28 September 2024.
22. "Response to City Council Motion MM11.37," Letter to Mayor Chow, Toronto Police Services Board, 2 November 2023.
23. Mahdis Habibinia, "Toronto seeing 'staggering' spike in hate-crime since Oct. 7, police chief says," *Toronto Star*, 23 November 2023.
24. Martin Lukacs, "Inside the 'shocking' police operation targeting pro-Palestinian activists in Toronto," *The Breach*, 17 June 2024.
25. Howard Levitt, "If your employer expresses sympathy for Hamas, here are your options," *Financial Post*, 13 October 2023.
26. Lukacs, "Inside the 'shocking' police operation."
27. Martin Lukacs, "Secretive committee in Ontario ministry pushed crackdown on pro-Palestine activism," *The Breach*, 27 June 2024.
28. Kunal Chaudhary, "Ontario government screened law students who signed pro-Palestine letter," *The Breach*, 21 December 2023.
29. The Honourable J. Michael MacDonald, "Strengthening the Pillars, Report of the TMU External Review," Toronto Metropolitan University, 31 May 2024.
30. "Trying to silence Yves Engler," *Blueprints of Disruption*, Episode 173, Podcast, 4 March 2025.
31. "I'm being charged for responding to anti-Palestinian hate on X," Yves Engler, 18 February 2025.
32. Sheldon Kirshner, "Pro-Palestinian Activism Spills into Antisemitism," *The Times of Israel*, 25 November 2023.
33. Faisal Kutty, "Drop the charges against Indigo Peace 11 protesters," *Al Jazeera*, 5 January 2024.

CHAPTER 5

What Being Pro-Palestine Means to Me

Sheima Benembarek

"Børn i Gaza har ret til et liv!"

It's a late November afternoon in 2023 in a gloomy Copenhagen, where I'm visiting friends for a few days, and the only reason I know what those Danish words mean is that I'm one of the protesters walking down H. C. Andersens Boulevard. I'm surrounded by a sea of bobbing heads covered in black and white checkered keffiyehs and raised arms waving Palestinian flags. There are thousands of us marching and chanting that, yes, children in Gaza have a right to life. Faces that look like mine acknowledge me with smiles of recognition, and kernels of Arabic pop around me with such frequency that I can't take them all in.

Some of the banners and placards are in English, and they read "Ceasefire now!" or "Stop the massacre!" or, one of my favourites, "Palestine will never die!" By the time we get to Christiansborg Palace square, it starts to rain, but no one seems to mind, and I haven't felt this kind of communal warmth in a long time.

I photograph a protester standing on the roof of a parked car, holding a glowing red flare in the air. As I prepare to post the image on Instagram, I look at my friends—one is Lebanese Canadian, one is Jordanian American—and ask, "Too much? Will people in Canada think I've been radicalized?" But I don't wait for their answers because I realize I don't like that I'm even asking these questions. I press "Share."

A few weeks prior, on October 8, 2023—the day after Hamas led an armed attack on Israel, resulting in the massacre of 1,200 and the abduction of 240 hostages, mostly civilians—my partner warned me, "Be careful what you say publicly right now." I knew what he meant and why that was the first thing he said to me when we learned of the news. But anyone who'd been paying attention to this issue knew what would follow: a brutal and merciless retaliation, eventually escalating to war and what many experts are now calling a genocide. For the first time in my adult life, I no longer cared whether expressing solidarity with the Palestinian people would affect my career or friendships.

That same day, I posted on Instagram a digital illustration of a young girl in front of a Palestinian flag, with the words "Free Palestine" in bold white letters above her. In the face of Israel's impending counterattack, my expression of support felt like a helpless plea. The Nakba, or catastrophe, refers to the forced and violent displacement of 750,000 Palestinians during the 1948 Arab-Israeli war. For 75 years, an entire people have been stripped of their human rights while living under occupation. The oppressive military system of rule has included policies of arbitrary punishment, land confiscations, and a goods blockade, altering every aspect of daily life such as mobility, association, and even access to electricity and clean water. There are roughly 7 million Palestinians in the diaspora. And when I say "Free Palestine," I mean that I want Palestinians to be afforded basic humanity, to have safety, autonomy, and dignity—all rights that Israel's military response has further obliterated in the name of eliminating Hamas.

But some see statements like this as threatening and offensive. A CBC piece, published on December 22, 2023, describes the "chilling effect" on professionals in various sectors who have expressed their support for Palestinians. On November 10, 2023, *The Maple* published a list of 17 people who had allegedly been fired for their pro-Palestine views, including Hamilton, Ontario, MPP Sarah Jama, who was ejected from the provincial NDP caucus. And so, for me, standing up for Palestinians in any way—even if it's only on social media—is meaningful, precisely because of these kinds of attempts at silencing.

When I immigrated from Morocco roughly twenty years ago, I studied at Montreal's Concordia University and made friends of different ethnicities and faiths. I quickly discovered that in Canada, censorship is enforced politely, indirectly. You learn to read the room. You change the subject when none of your Canadian friends say anything as you bring up Palestinian resistance over dinner, when the mood becomes tense and you realize you and "the Palestine issue" are a bummer. Now, staying silent to avoid trouble feels painful, if not cowardly.

But months into the war, I can't shake off the feeling that, somehow, I'm being censored—even if it's a default self-censorship. That if I want to continue succeeding in this country, and especially in the journalism industry, I need to think long and hard about what and who I admit I am aligned with. This is the first time I put words on paper articulating these complicated thoughts and feelings and submit them for publication in a national outlet. I know others who understandably still don't want to take the risk of a public backlash.

While I can't remember the exact date, I have a vivid memory of my family sitting in front of the TV in Morocco, transfixed by the news of Palestinians being attacked once again during Ramadan. My mother crying. My father's eyebrows furrowed. The rhetorical question that no one asked out loud: Why could we break our fast in peace and they couldn't? At the time, I didn't understand the depth of my parents' feelings; I also didn't know yet that while my family calls it Palestine, it's not officially recognized by the majority of the world as a country. But I gathered that these people are my people too. That their pain is our pain. We're one ummah.

October 7, 2023, was a day of horror. Of course, I care about the trauma that was inflicted on Israeli civilians and Jews around the world, and I empathize with their suffering. But history has been good at repeating itself when it comes to Palestinians. This is why I am pulled towards expressing worry about their plight and why I am for their resistance.

It's obvious that for my Arab and Jewish friends, focusing on work is almost impossible. I keep in touch with one of my close friends, a Jewish woman, more than usual. We get on the phone when the words in text messages just don't cut it, don't carry the feelings of woe and helplessness. We lament about how it's suddenly so hard to talk to people, to connect. We're both grateful that we understand each other. I ask her directly whether she feels insulted by my "Free Palestine" Instagram post. "I know you, so no. But I can see how it might land badly with others," she replies.

I fly back to Montreal days after the protest in Copenhagen and make my way to the Eastern Townships, where I live. In this small Franco-Canadian town of roughly 11,000 people, the only other Arabs I've come across are two young Moroccan men who work at the lone McDonald's. When I go in for a Big Mac after my return to Canada, they smile in recognition and call me "sister." I've gone back after that specifically to say hi. I don't verbalize to anyone the loneliness I experience while thinking about what will come of the Palestinians in Gaza when I'm one of the only visible Arabs in town. I'm reminded that I still haven't figured out how to maintain community in this country that replicates the feeling of belonging I have when I go back for a visit to Morocco.

The divisive, emotional reactions to social media statements of Palestinian support can also lead to broken friendships; I've experienced this myself, and I know others have too. The current atmosphere reminds me of the height of the pandemic, when so many of us felt compelled to declare our allegiance. Pro-mask or anti-mask? Vaccinated or anti-vaxxer? Then, like today, you were either on one side or the other, and your friends either thought like you did or they were no longer your friends. I wonder if we'll ever be able to think beyond taking sides. If being pro-justice and equity will ever feel less lonely.

Meanwhile, as of August 2025, over 62,000 Palestinians have been killed in Gaza, the majority of them women and children, according to the Gaza Health Ministry. The British medical journal *The Lancet* says that number is many degrees higher.[1] A UN human rights report puts the death toll for journalists at 247 as of the end of August, 2025.[2] According to *Al Jazeera*, who lost 10 of their own reporters, that number is as high as 278. It is the deadliest conflict for journalists ever documented, according to the Committee to Protect Journalists. The UN has "irrefutably" confirmed that Gaza is now gripped by famine, and aid agencies report being obstructed from delivering food and medical supplies. The images and reports coming out of Rafah, where hundreds of thousands of displaced people have taken refuge, are haunting.

I don't know what liberation for Palestinians will look like, or if I'll see it in my lifetime. But I do know that the fear of speaking up is no match for the grief of silence. And I've decided I'd rather risk discomfort—and potentially losing work opportunities—any day than betray my own sense of justice.

Notes

1. Zeina Jamaluddine, et al, *The Lancet*, Volume 405, Issue, 10477, 8 February 2025.
2. "Killing of journalists in Gaza hospital attack 'should shock the world': UN rights office," *UN News*, 26 August 2025.

CHAPTER 6

From Bombs to Bullies: The Hounding of Fred Hahn

Robin Philpot

When Ontario Premier Doug Ford calls someone a "bully," a "disgusting human being," and a "terrible man" and asks that he be removed from his elected position, it is an affront to anyone who takes free speech, democracy, and freedom seriously. Particularly trade unionists.

Fred Hahn was the target of that attack by Doug Ford on August 21, 2024. Hahn, president of the Canadian Union of Public Employees (CUPE) Ontario and General Vice President of CUPE Canada, is the elected leader of some 300,000 CUPE members. The day before, Ford's labour minister David Piccini had accosted Hahn and accused him of being an antisemite.

Both Ford and Piccini are in the loud and powerful section of a chorus that includes—alas—the National Executive Board of CUPE. On the very day Piccini accosted Fred Hahn, the CUPE National Board adopted a resolution asking Fred Hahn to resign as General Vice-President of CUPE.

What was the "crime" that earned Fred Hahn such insults from people in power and prompted his own union to bury basic trade union principles such as freedom of speech, due process, democracy, and respect for the choices of rank-and-file union members?

They claimed it was because he shared an AI-generated cartoon-type video on social media of an Israeli Olympic diver doing somersaults from the board then turning into a bomb as he hits the water. The real answer, however, is that Fred Hahn has steadfastly supported Palestinian resistance since he became an active trade unionist. He has often said, "It was the members of the union who educated me about Palestine." He has not wavered in his support, which is why pro-Israel groups in Canada have for years striven—in vain—to silence him with unfounded accusations.

Hahn's response to the attacks has been unequivocal. "I want to be clear," he stated, "I utterly reject the charge of antisemitism; anyone who knows and works with me knows it to be a lie. It remains my strongly held view that it is a terrible mistake, and antisemitic, to conflate abhorrent actions by the state of Israel with Jewish humanity or identity."

In response to the CUPE National Board's request that he resign, Hahn said, "Trade unionists I have come to know and respect voted this week to overturn the democratic decisions of CUPE members. It is unprecedented in our union's history and I'm worried countless CUPE members who are active in the Palestinian solidarity movement could be left more vulnerable and exposed by the precedent as they face similar situations as work."

Turning courts into propaganda tools

The stage had been well set for Doug Ford's outbursts. On October 8, 2023, a small coordinated group of CUPE members, piloted by Conservative lawyer Kathryn Marshall, filed complaints before the Ontario Human Rights Tribunal. They criticized Fred Hahn for an October 7 tweet in which he said he was "thankful" for the "power of resistance around the globe. Because resistance is fruitful and no matter what some say, resistance brings progress, and for that I am thankful." Hahn apologized shortly thereafter.

But the sweeping allegations before the Human Rights Tribunal go much further. They allege the union has been guilty of discrimination and antisemitism, not only after October 7, 2023, but also for many years before. Allegations include the "promoting and passing antisemitic union resolutions," and distributing documentation claiming Israel is "ethically cleansing" the Palestinian people. Other accusations include

- CUPE adopted a resolution in 2018 stating that "Israel was 'illegally' occupying Palestine."
- The 2021 CUPE National Convention called "on the Canadian government to exert pressure on Israel and pushed support for the BDS campaign."
- A 2023 emergency resolution at the CUPE national convention states that CUPE will conduct "member education" about the history of Israel's "occupation and colonization" of Palestine, including Canada's "complicity," and what trade unions can do.
- In 2023 a CUPE Ontario resolution to reject the International Holocaust Remembrance Alliance's

definition of antisemitism. (Many countries, many unions and many Jewish organizations have also rejected that definition.)

In addition to an indemnity of $500,000 for their "pain and suffering," the complainants demanded the right to "re-direct their union dues to a Jewish charity of their choice." The goal is obviously to cripple the union.

Considering Israel's live-streamed indiscriminate and massive killing in Gaza, its forced displacement and starving of Palestinians since 2023, and its deliberate assassination of journalists, a serious tribunal would dismiss such a flimsy complaint immediately. Adjudicators would know that to rule in the complainants' favour would set a precedent that could be used against thousands of people and hundreds of organizations, including the Canadian Labour Congress, UNIFOR (see above), and even the Prime Minister of Canada.

CUPE and Fred Hahn are guilty only of being perceptive, far-sighted, and, above all, right on the war on Gaza. If more people in power had taken heed, there might have been more action to put an end to the genocide.

CUPE's efforts to have the Tribunal dismiss the complaints have been thwarted by lawyer Kathryn Marshall and her clients. She and her backers want to keep the complaint—and the damning accusations—alive for propaganda purposes. They know that media and political opinion will preface all discussion about Fred Hahn, CUPE, and Palestine, by referencing the allegations of antisemitism and presuming Hahn guilty until proven innocent. Another way to punish solidarity and dissent in Canada for those who raise the issue of Palestine.

Trade unionists have every reason to be suspicious about Kathryn Marshall and her clients' motives in initiating this case. Marshall comes from rabid anti-union, right-wing tradition, proudly calling her firm "MARSHALL LAW." On August 3, 2025, on X (@lawsome), she boasted about another case, reported in the *Toronto Star*, in which she is championing a few disgruntled teachers' union members in an aim to divide and break the union: "At Marshall Law," she tweeted, "we love front pages. We also love fighting unions."

Fred Hahn adheres to the guiding principles of trade unionism

The frenzy whipped up by Doug Ford and others about Fred Hahn forces us to reflect on the principles of trade unionism in a danger-fraught and rapidly changing world. The International Longshore and Warehouse Union (ILWU) has often been at the forefront of international solidarity actions, including refusal to load ships headed to countries conducting wars, and notably Apartheid South Africa. In 1953 in San Francisco, the union adopted "Ten Guiding Principles of the ILWU." Adopted widely throughout the world, the cardinal principles include the following.

- Members make up unions and are the best judge of their own welfare. It is not up to officers, employers, politicians, or self-assigned "experts" to decide for them.

- Members openly debate the burning issues and decide democratically on the path to take.
- Members freely elect their leaders and representatives and are the only ones who can remove them.
- Discrimination based on race, colour, creed, national origin, religious or political belief, sex, gender preference, or sexual orientation cannot be tolerated. Worker unity is essential.
- Helping workers in distress is the job of all trade unions and members. That's what solidarity is about.
- Workers throughout the world have the same basic aspirations. International solidarity is fundamental and necessary to defend the interests of workers and their unions domestically and internationally.

By any measure, Fred Hahn and CUPE Ontario have abided by union principles and have provided leadership for others, specifically with regards to Palestine. They deserve credit and solidarity, not back-stabbing.

The resolution by CUPE's National Executive Board asking Hahn to resign was a very unfortunate mistake. Not only did the Board break with the fundamental principles it supposedly defends—free speech and democracy—but it also weakened the union as a whole by contravening its own constitution, sowing division, and casting doubt among members on its own commitment to this and other issues. If a leader makes mistakes, it's up to those who elected him or her to decide. In short, the Board has tied itself in a knot that is not easy to untie.

Fred Hahn and CUPE are not alone

The strident attacks on Ontario CUPE and its leader for simply speaking out cannot eclipse the fact that unions throughout the world are displaying a new militant international solidarity with the Palestinian people.

True to tradition, longshore workers appear to be leading the way. San Francisco Bay area longshore workers members of the ILWU, UAW, and other unions have led, supported, and participated in blockades to prevent ships from loading and unloading cargo to and from Israel. (*Labor Notes*, 5 March 2024)

In August, 2025, according to *Press TV*, Belgian port-workers' unions refused to provide services to airlines flying from Brussels to Tel Aviv. In a release, they declared, "Since October 2023, a genocide has been underway in Gaza and the West Bank against the Palestinian population. Serious violations of humanitarian and international law continue. Despite this, some airlines have decided to resume flights to Tel Aviv. Our affiliates refuse to participate in these operations. We will not provide services to these flights."

In June, 2025, at the Charles-de-Gaulle airport in Paris, unions refused to load military material in planes flying to Israel. The Force Ouvrière Air France local declared: "Air transport workers must not be part of the death machine currently raging in Gaza. We oppose the transport of military equipment that would contribute to the ongoing genocide." He insisted that "air transport must be used for vital humanitarian aid for the children, women, and men of Gaza." (*20minutes*, 14 June 2025)

At France's huge Fos-sur-Mer port near Marseille, longshore workers refused to load a large ammunition shipment headed to Israel. They refused to participate in "the genocide being conducted by the Israeli government." (*20minutes*, 14 June 2025)

Greek dockworkers at Piraeus, Greece's largest port, have been in the forefront of this international wave of solidarity with Palestine, issuing this statement:

> Our unions have been making it clear since October 2023 that as employees of the Organization of the Port of Piraeus, we declare our full support and express our solidarity with the Palestinian People. The escalation of the blind violence and destruction taking place in Gaza causes us only horror and disgust. (. . .) We declare in all directions that the employees of the Piraeus Port Authority do not accept to serve any cargo, any ship, we will not provide any facility that will supply military material to Israel. (*Mena Solidarity Network*, 10 July 2025)

At the time of writing, the Canadian Labour Congress (CLC) representing upwards of three million workers had recently called on Canada to support an arms embargo on Israel, to continue funding UN agencies including UNRWA, impose targeted sanctions, cancel the Canada-Israel Free Trade Agreement, and prohibit all trade with illegal Israel settlements.

Unifor, the largest private sector union in Canada, had just adopted a resolution at its convention calling for an arms embargo on Israel, endorsing the Palestine civil society call for boycott, divestment, and sanctions (BDS) as "the only reasonable course of action to end the genocide in Palestine." Unifor also awarded its highest honour, The Nelson Mandela Award, to the Palestinian Journalists' Syndicate represented by its President Naser Abubaker in recognition of media workers' dangerous and unrelenting coverage of the conflict in Gaza. Majd Samaroo, a representative of the Palestinian General Federation of Trade Unions was also a guest at the Convention. When she was introduced at the Women's Caucus lunch, she received a standing ovation.

Yet, Fred Hahn and CUPE are dragged over the coals and punished for statements of solidarity with Palestine. The question to Doug Ford remains: Are all these workers "disgusting human beings," "bullies," and "terrible" people?

PART TWO

RADIO SILENCE

CHAPTER 7

Silence. One Second. Five Seconds.

Arfa Rana

> I chose journalism to be close to people.
> It might not be easy to change the reality,
> but at least I can bring their voice to the world.
>
> —Shireen Abu Akleh, 1971-2022

I was 20 years old when veteran Palestinian-American journalist Shireen Abu Akleh was shot and killed in May 2022 while on duty, still wearing her navy-blue press helmet and vest. While Akleh's death caused an uproar for a few weeks across international headlines, she soon disappeared into the abyss of dead news.

Akleh was a symbol for everything a journalist embodies. She was a woman who served the cause of her people despite being subjected to the permanent threat of violence by Israel, the IDF, and Israeli settlers. Her life was fuelled by a moral courage to report the truth in a world willingly deceived by lies. But Akleh's murder by an IDF sniper was also a chilling reminder of the price one pays to lift a mirror to the face of imperialists and reveal the ugliness of the occupier's lies.

When I landed my dream job at CBC after graduating from university in 2023, I entered those glass doors with purpose. I held Akleh's story in my heart and promised to honour not only her legacy, but all those around the world who have been martyred for their truth-telling. I silently vowed that I would report and share stories the way they were meant to be told: with raw emotion, inconvenient truths, and fingers pointing to those that should be held accountable. I believed this was universally understood to be the journalistic creed.

I began as a temporary reporter on the East Coast in New Brunswick. Every day was a new adventure as I got accustomed to the fast-paced newsrooms and tight deadlines. But by the end of that summer, I missed home and decided to transfer to another CBC newsroom in Ontario to be close to my family.

At CBC London, a glass wall separated my desk from the outside world. For most of the day, phones would be ringing, a dozen tabs would be open on my desktop to keep an eye out for news, and, by the afternoon, a stressful silence would overtake the newsroom as we approached our afternoon deadlines. It was the life I wanted.

Sometimes, I would glance outside the window in the heart of downtown London, ON, and lose myself in the faces outside. I watched a man in tattered clothing and disheveled hair spot a half-eaten sandwich on the ground and bite into it hungrily; I saw a woman nestled under a blanket as a police officer roused her; and, once, paramedics took away a limp body shrouded in white cloth in the early hours of a winter morning. What were their stories? It was unimaginable that somebody died on the streets and yet, the world remained unmoved, unchanged, indifferent. It was telling me something.

CBC is a public broadcaster whose authority lies in being Canada's central source of information. Yet its pattern of disassociation and editorial bias and complacency echoed through major international stories, particularly on Israel and Palestine. The weekend of October 7, 2023, we watched as Palestinian resistance fighters tore through the 30-year-old apartheid wall surrounding Gaza and broke free into Israeli settlements—land that had been theirs, even homes that they recognized from childhood. Panic erupted in CBC newsrooms as senior reporters scrambled to their desks and veteran journalists were deployed to Israel and the West Bank. The next day Israel began its carpet bombing of Palestinians. But while the lives of Palestinians in Gaza would never be the same again, journalism at the CBC would continue unbothered.

The following Monday, I sat in the familiar circle of faces for our morning meeting. I was the only Muslim in the office. The executive producer, Anna (not her real name) admonished me: "We are going to let the facts tell the story. Not our emotions." But I never presumed or said otherwise. When it was my turn to talk, my heart nearly exploded out of my chest, the way it does when I am afraid I might be misunderstood.

I reminded them that America's so-called War on Terror and the sensationalized hunt for "weapons of mass destruction" after 9/11 disproportionally affected Muslims and Arabs, both abroad and in the diaspora. My biggest fear was that we would recreate this hysteria through our reporting. More than ever, I told them, it was vital to include the historical context of Israel's settler-colonial violence to this eruption. Otherwise, the world would dehumanize the Palestinians even more, thinking October 7 was a single, isolated event. And who would pay the price? The Palestinians in Gaza, and all Muslims and Arabs in North America. The same way events played out in 2003.

Silence. One second. Five seconds. Anna eventually said there is a "team of experts on the Middle East" working around the clock to ensure our coverage is accurate and so I "don't need to worry."

As she spoke, the large flat-screen TV on the newsroom's opposing walls, playing CBC news 24/7, shouted its headline in big letters: "Hamas Attacks."

By the end of the week, Anna called me into the office for a check-in about how I had been doing. I told her that although I was fine, I was gravely concerned about CBC's ongoing coverage of Israel. The meeting was long and Anna reminded me that CBC's policy was to report the facts, which included both the Israeli and the Palestinian perspective. I asked why CBC was advocating for "both sides" when one was clearly a wealthy colonizer and the other was the impoverished oppressed. As if they were equals?

I was dismissed from morning pitch meetings. Instead, before I even reached my desk, Anna would have stories assigned to me. Although the newsroom made an effort to interview Palestinians and gave them space to share their story, it was never enough and it was never contextual. Meanwhile, criticism of Western reporting only grew stronger around the world. My feed on social media was filled with videos and images of decapitated bodies, parents carrying their children in plastic bags, and long lines of the sick, elderly, and amputees travelling from the north of Gaza to the south, getting shot and bombed along the way.

Near the end of 2023, a CBC executive, Eli (not her real name) visited our local newsroom. I booked a short meeting with her, repeating the same concerns that I had confided in Anna. I reminded her that CBC had played a role in sensationalizing the false story about Hamas beheading 40 Israeli babies; yet when the IDF and then *The New York Times* confirmed that had not been true, the story dissipated without clarification or apology. I was exhausted from repeating myself again and again: *This is exactly how the Americans justified the invasion of Iraq. If objectivity is reporting the facts, why aren't we telling the truth?*

Eli explained that with all major international stories, it takes a while for the storm to settle and the truth to come out. She reassured me that my voice and opinions mattered, that I was not hired at CBC to write only about the food and music of BIPOC communities—an odd comment, seeing as I was hired as a news reporter. She suggested I seek out the mental health services offered by CBC—but I didn't need mental health services. I needed CBC to deliver the factual information they promised their audience.

CBC has a glossary on the Middle East, a vocabulary list CBC journalists are expected to use when reporting on Israel and Palestine. For example, the Language Guide discourages referring to the separation barrier between Israel and the West Bank as an act of apartheid, despite the International Court of Justice calling the wall illegal in 2004. According to the Guide, the Gaza Strip is "technically not occupied" even though "Israel largely controls all movement in and out." The country of Palestine is non-existent, "although there's a movement to establish one as part of a two-state peace agreement with Israel."

The language CBC uses and the narratives it paints is deliberate. In conversations with CBC journalists across different newsrooms, I was told that some editors made a point of reserving the terms "slaughter," "massacre," and "brutal" only for attacks against Israeli settlers and rarely ever towards Israeli attacks against Palestinians.

Every few weeks after October 7, editor-in-chief Brodie Fenlon would mass email all CBC staff with updates on CBC's coverage on Israel and Palestine. In one email, Fenlon wrote: "We do not post or share to ANY social media platform information that CBC has not—or would not—put on air or online. That includes information we have not verified or are not reporting ourselves as CBC News, even when it comes from external news sources."

Considering that CBC did not have a reporter based in Gaza, and the majority of the primary news sources CBC relied on were directly from the Israeli government, it was laughable that Canada's public broadcaster made the professional decision to disregard the voices of Palestinians, particularly Palestinian journalists (who died in larger numbers than journalists in any other conflict).

When they did speak to Palestinians, grief and anger was not given context, such as the story behind this trauma-porn headline: "Palestinian-Canadian man mourns 29 dead family members."

My experience as a reporter at CBC showed me how Western newsrooms pulsate with the privilege of power and authority. While CBC may be considered a progressive media outlet, it produces "diversity" stories only as long as they align with colonial narratives. Stories of loss, trauma, and culture in marginalized communities are often amplified, while those exploring the colonial legacies of nations in the Global South and their diasporas are too complex or ignored.

What particularly frustrated me is that when I questioned the Language Guide or criticized Fenlon's statements, I was never granted clarification of CBC's actual editorial decisions. Demanding answers and advocating for Palestinian perspectives was a soul-sucking battle. Well before the Palestinian death toll reached 20,000 in March 2024, anyone could see that the destruction in Gaza was far from the "Israeli-Hamas" war, but was a clear case of ethnic cleansing. Bombing hospitals, destroying UN schools, targeting refugee camps, and killing media workers undermine international law and violate basic human rights. Yet, as long as the CBC Language Guide instructed journalists to refer to Israel's bombardment as the "Israel-Hamas war," CBC staff followed with their heads bowed, no questions asked.

I decided to leave CBC in June, 2024. In a short email with no explanations, I gave notice that I would no longer be working at CBC two weeks hence. I considered voicing my stance on Palestine once more, critiquing the Language Guide one last time, or pleading with my colleagues that they at least make an effort to understand the complexity of the Gaza genocide. But I decided against it. After all, if CBC wasn't afraid of telling the truth, wouldn't things have changed by now?

In the months that followed, my conscience tugged at my moral obligation. I am a journalist. I had seen the flaws of CBC's reporting from the inside, while Canadians remain unaware of the decision to perpetuate a white-washed version of Israel's crimes against humanity.

In October 2025, I published an exposé in *Mondoweiss* titled "I resigned from Canada's largest broadcasting corporation over its complicity in Israel's genocide." This prompted a slew of emails from both current and former CBC journalists who had similar experiences. Some were inspired to resign after my article, while others continue to resist and fight for better coverage on Palestine.

This summer, five more journalists were killed, bombed in a "double strike" on a hospital that left 21 dead, including health workers and the rescue crew. As of the end of August, 2025, the UN counts the total number of journalists killed at 247.

The IDF cannot fathom that killing a journalist does not erase their existence or even their stories. Many CBC reporters, afraid of Israeli lobby groups such as Honest Reporting Canada or doxxing lists found on the Canary Mission website, shield themselves from backlash by complying with the oppressors.

Canadian journalism needs to be rewired to uphold new standards that reflect integrity, true objectivity, and, above all, honesty. Truth, after all, is the best revenge. It travels through the minds of all those who hold a conscience, ruining the sleep of the privileged in power.

CHAPTER 8

The Elephant in the Newsroom: The Palestinian Exception at CTV

Yara Jamal

I was hired by CTV on September 12, 2022, and soon after felt like an elephant in the room—the one whose presence was met with quiet discomfort, unacknowledged tension, and unspoken questions.

I had a coaster on my desk, a gift from a friend, that featured a keffiyeh pattern and the word *Haifa*. One day, an editor, who also happened to be my union representative, asked me what it said. I explained that Haifa was where my family was from. She countered that *Haifa is an Israeli city.* As if she had the authority to dictate my identity. As if my own history, my family's history, was hers to rewrite. I told her that *Haifa is a Palestinian city and I am a Palestinian woman.* She walked away, casually adding that she had visited Haifa and found it to be "*so* beautiful."

Here was this woman, a white editor with over a decade of experience in the media, yet she lacked the most basic awareness or sensitivity to recognize the weight of her words. Of course, Haifa is beautiful. But how would I know? I have never been allowed to see it, nor did my grandfather ever see it again once he was exiled. This is what people fail to recognize: how tone-deaf interactions like this, seemingly small and inconsequential, contribute to the larger erasure of Palestine. These everyday conversations, in their sheer disregard for Palestinian existence, succeed in removing us from our own narrative. They reinforce the idea that our history is up for debate and that our pain is something to be dismissed or ignored.

A few months later, I was told I'd be taking on the role of a writer, which included creating a bio for the CTV website. In the bio I submitted, I stated that I was from Haifa, Palestine. For my colleagues, getting their bios published took only a few hours or days. Despite multiple follow-ups, mine was delayed without explanation. While coworkers could freely include their hometowns, I wasn't given the same leeway. When it was finally published—after weeks of unexplained delay—the word *Palestine* had been removed.

One afternoon, a 6 o'clock news host struck up a conversation and asked where I was from. *Palestine*, I answered. A brief pause. A palpable, awkward silence. He quickly pivoted into a story about reporting in Jerusalem and "Israel."

Once again, my existence was the elephant in the room. My identity as a Palestinian had been handed to him and instead of engaging with it, he deflected, shifting the conversation away from me and back into the framework that the media so carefully upholds—one where Israel is central and Palestine is either erased or spoken about in passing, without depth, without history, without humanity.

I had to wonder: was all this ignorance? Was it discomfort? Were these deliberate microaggressions, attempts to provoke me into reacting? Because here, even in a newsroom where the expectation of information and history should be a given, Palestine was not a given. Palestine was not part of the conversation. Palestine *is* the exception—always treated as a taboo, an unspoken subject, something too dangerous to acknowledge, too controversial to speak of. Incidents like these highlight the deep biases within mainstream media. They are not just accidental; they are reflective of a larger, systemic disregard for Palestinian narratives and rights.

It became evident that many journalists around me lacked the information, integrity, or courage to challenge Zionist narratives. But, as I would soon discover, this wasn't just about individual ignorance or bias—it was about institutional complicity.

CTV and the Institutional Erasure of Palestine

Bell Media, the parent company of CTV, made its alignment with Zionist interests clear early on.

Internal emails obtained by *The Breach* exposed how in November, 2023, CTV actively censored reporting on Palestine. Journalists were explicitly instructed not to use the word *Palestine* and were even directed to claim that "Palestine...does not currently exist." This directive—issued on October 10—though framed as a necessary editorial standard, was in actuality a blatant political statement. As *The Breach* revealed, Bell Media made it clear that these were non-negotiable talking points:

> "Given radically conflicting viewpoints and the sensitive nature of the current situation in the Middle East, this note is not to be circulated externally," wrote *CTV News* assignment editor Mark Khouzam. "While Palestine has observer status at the United Nations, Palestine as a nation does not currently exist. Please use Gaza or the Israeli Occupied West Bank for a geographic locator."

This is a textbook example of an institution actively participating in the erasure of an occupied and oppressed people. It is a direct order to journalists to conform to an ideological narrative that upholds Israel's settler-colonial project while denying Palestinians even the right to name their homeland.

But a precedent had already been set. In 2021, CBC News had issued a nearly identical directive, instructing its journalists not to use the word *Palestine*, claiming that "there is no modern country of Palestine." Employees were warned not to include the word even in drafts or internal discussions.

These directives are not just acts of linguistic manipulation; they are acts of violence. When media institutions erase the very name of a people, they participate in their dispossession. This level of censorship exposes a Western media landscape that masquerades as objective but is, in reality, deeply compromised and controlled. This is not journalism. This is propaganda.

Censoring Palestine: Erasure in the Newsroom

One of my roles at CTV was as a production assistant, where I was responsible for reviewing and editing scripts. Before October 7, 2023, Palestine was barely, if ever, on

CTV's radar, typical of most mainstream media outlets. But in the aftermath, as stories began trickling in, I noticed a pattern: the use of terms like *the Palestine-Israel conflict,* and Israeli casualties were *killed,* while Palestinians were simply *dead*—as if their lives had ended without cause and their deaths required no explanation.

Each time I came across these distortions, I made a point of correcting them. I explained to producers and hosts why their phrasing was not only misleading but deeply dehumanizing. My supervisors and producers rarely acknowledged my edits directly, but their silence and discomfort spoke volumes. They weren't just uninterested in journalistic integrity—they were actively complicit in its erosion.

Western media is not afraid of inaccuracy—it thrives on it. What it fears is truth, diversity, and inclusion. It ensures its survival by keeping newsroom leadership overwhelmingly white and picking underqualified white individuals who will toe the line dictated by Zionist lobbies.

The Cost of Challenging the Narrative

On October 17, 2023, the Al-Ahli Arab Hospital in Gaza suffered a horrific attack that killed hundreds of children and families seeking refuge and medical care. I learned of this atrocity while preparing for the 6 o'clock broadcast. Sitting in the cramped control room, headset on, I watched the news unfold. As the story about the hospital bombing aired, a suffocating tension filled the room. I could hear every word spoken by my colleagues over their microphones. One co-worker questioned why Hamas would target civilians and lamented why "both sides" couldn't just get along.

Those two minutes while the story played felt interminable. I sat there, the only Palestinian in the room, trying to process the news of a massacre of my people while also enduring a conversation that reduced their suffering to a backdrop for misguided commentary.

That moment encapsulated the reality of the "Palestine Exception"—the complete lack of acknowledgement, let alone empathy, for Palestinian humanity. It was as if the room had become deaf to the pain of what had just been reported. The casual dismissal of Palestinian lives, juxtaposed with the moral outrage reserved only for others, was a stark reminder of how deeply rooted this bias is in Western institutions.

After the bombing of the hospital, the slaughter in Gaza reached a new peak. I texted my supervisor to let her know I would be attending rallies and vigils because my community, and I, were in mourning. I told her how deeply this tragedy was affecting us.

On October 22, 2023, I held a rally in solidarity with those grieving in Gaza. During the event, a journalist from the SaltWire Network (a now defunct Halifax newspaper publisher, acquired by Postmedia in 2024) approached me for an interview. I agreed but declined to identify myself for safety reasons. In the interview, he asked if Jews could exist in a free Palestine. I answered, and still stand by my words: "Jews have always existed in Palestine. This isn't a religious war. Jews can continue to exist, but the Zionist ideology cannot."

When the article was published, the journalist not only distorted my words, he included my full name. An onslaught of trolls quickly seized on the misrepresentation, stripping my quote of its context and amplifying it into a viral Twitter thread. The headline, "Jews can continue to exist, but the Zionist ideology cannot," was now twisted to label me as "antisemitic." As if coordinated, these posts tagged both CTV and Bell Media. By the time the tweets went viral, I knew I would be fired.

The next day, I was called into my manager's office. I explained the situation, emphasizing that I had never revealed where I worked or my name during the rally, and that my supervisor was aware of my involvement. I also reaffirmed that I stood by my comments and that they were not offensive.

He said that as journalists we are required to be "impartial." The irony wasn't lost on me when he asked if I agreed with the supposedly antisemitic statement that characterized Hamas's attacks as acts of resistance. If impartiality was truly the standard, why was I being questioned on whether I viewed Hamas's actions as resistance or terrorism? It was clear this wasn't about impartiality—it was about silencing me as a Palestinian journalist.

The meeting ended with my manager saying a thorough investigation would follow. Five hours later, he called again and asked me to return the next day, as the investigation had already concluded.

I was let go.

Immediately after, my union representative filed a grievance as it was clear that I was being fired not for any professional misconduct, but for who I am and what I represent as a Palestinian journalist. After the grievance, we went to an arbitration hearing a few months later, where the matter was resolved.

The Manufactured Ignorance of Western Journalism

Working in the CTV newsroom was an eye-opener. It confirmed how deeply compromised Western journalism is, and how journalists are often required to be puppets of corporate interests. While I had anticipated a certain amount of editorial bias, what raised serious red flags was the profound ignorance encountered among my colleagues—people you'd assume to be informed, given their profession.

I vividly recall conversations with seasoned journalists, some with over a decade of experience at CTV and in the industry. More than once, after pointing out that misleading language was being used to report on the Gaza genocide, I would hear that they are "unfamiliar with what's happening in that part of the world."

How can a journalist report on a story involving genocide without even attempting to even grasp the fundamentals of its background? Ignorance in journalism is not a neutral phenomenon—it is complicity. And the ignorance I encountered at CTV wasn't just personal; it was systemic. It reflected the broader culture of mainstream media, which prioritizes sanitized narratives over uncomfortable truths.

IHRA Definition: A Shield for Israel

One of the most insidious tools used to suppress and misconstrue the Palestinian narrative is the International Holocaust Remembrance Alliance (IHRA) definition of antisemitism. First devised in 2016, this definition was strategically formulated to shield Israel from criticism and makes no contribution to protecting Jewish people from actual discrimination. Instead, it is a politically motivated tool used to punish those who speak out against apartheid and ethnic cleansing. Seven out of the 11 examples provided within the IHRA framework conflate legitimate criticism of Israel with antisemitism—an intentional distortion designed to criminalize Palestinian advocacy and silence the truth about Israeli atrocities toward the Palestinians.

The IHRA definition also perpetuates a systemic environment where violence against Palestinians is normalized and justified. By framing criticism of Israel as antisemitism, it erases the diversity of the Palestinian identity and experience, as well as their entire history.

The consequences of adopting the IHRA definition have been severe. In 2019, Kenneth Stern—the original author of the IHRA definition—condemned its use in academic spaces. He testified before the US Congress that its implementation would have a "chilling effect" on free speech, a fear echoed by academics worldwide, including Jewish scholars. A year-long study by University College London in 2020 concluded that the IHRA definition created a hostile academic environment, making students and faculty "anxious" about discussing Palestine and Israel.

Yet, despite these warnings, Western governments and institutions have adopted the IHRA definition, effectively legalizing a modern-day McCarthyism against Palestinians and their allies across a range of institutions and settings.

One is forced to ask why it is acceptable—encouraged, even—to condemn human rights abuses in China, Russia, or Iran, but unacceptable to criticize Israel's occupation, war crimes, and ethnic cleansing? The answer is simple: because exposing these truths threatens the carefully constructed Western narrative that allows Israel to act with impunity.

For nearly 80 years, Israel has engaged in ethnic cleansing, military occupation, and systemic oppression of the Palestinian people. The world must recognize the facts behind these crimes—not the distorted, whitewashed version promoted by Israeli apologists. The IHRA definition stands in direct opposition to the democratic principles of freedom of speech, academic integrity, and political accountability. It must be exposed for what it truly is: a tool of oppression, designed to silence the oppressed and shield the oppressor.

Anti-Palestinian Racism: A Necessary Term

Anti-Palestinian racism is the term that captures the discrimination and silencing faced by Palestinians. When I was fired, many described it as an "Islamophobic" or "anti-Arab" incident. While these terms address significant forms of discrimination, they fail to encapsulate the unique experience of Palestinians. My firing wasn't about my religion—I've never disclosed my religious or spiritual affiliations publicly—and it wasn't about being Arab. It was about being Palestinian.

The erasure and punishment of Palestinian identity and history is a core component of anti-Palestinian racism. In April 2022, the Arab Canadian Lawyers Association (ACLA) published a formal definition of anti-Palestinian racism, stating:

Anti-Palestinian racism is a form of anti-Arab racism that silences, excludes, erases, stereotypes, defames, or dehumanizes Palestinians or their narratives. Anti-Palestinian racism takes various forms, including:

1. Denying the Nakba and justifying violence against Palestinians;
2. Failing to acknowledge Palestinians as an Indigenous people with a collective identity, belonging, and rights in relation to occupied and historic Palestine;
3. Erasing the human rights and equal dignity and worth of Palestinians;
4. Excluding or pressuring others to exclude Palestinian perspectives, Palestinians, and their allies;
5. Defaming Palestinians and their allies with slander, such as being inherently antisemitic, a terrorist threat/sympathizer, or opposed to democratic values.

No Comfort for the Oppressor: Speaking Truth to Power

Every time I say, "I am Palestinian," I resist the erasure that has been systematically imposed on us. I reclaim the narrative and assert the legitimacy of my people's struggle. While the weight of being the elephant in the room can be exhausting, it is also a powerful position, one that demands attention, confronts bias, and insists on our right to exist and be heard.

The discomfort I evoke as the elephant in the room is not mine to resolve; it belongs to those who are unwilling to confront their own biases and the realities of Palestinian oppression. My role is not to make others comfortable—it's to speak the truth, to educate, and to advocate for our right to self-determination, sovereignty, and right of return.

By acknowledging both anti-Palestinian racism and pro-Israeli biases, we can shift the narrative. Instead of being the elephant in the room, Palestinians can take their rightful place in the conversation—as equals, as advocates, and as a people with a rich history and an undeniable right to self-determination.

CHAPTER 9

Do You See What They See: Gen Z and the New Media

Iman Kassam

After nearly two years of Israel's war on Gaza, Canada's major newsrooms are finally telling their audiences that Palestinians are starving. Stories now mention the spectre of a man-made famine; some even use the word "genocide." At first glance, it appears to be a long-overdue course correction. For many young Canadians, however, the damage is done. A generation raised with the world's images at its fingertips has concluded that legacy media cannot be trusted.

As part of my master's research last year, I interviewed nine Generation Z Canadians about their relationship with news. They didn't start from a place of blind trust, but October 7 and its aftermath marked a turning point. Hamas's attacks in Israel that day, and Israel's devastating military response in Gaza, dominated world headlines—yet both unfolded against a 78-year-long backdrop of occupation and resistance that news coverage rarely made room to explain.

Around the world, people watched livestreams of civilians killed, Instagram reels of hospitals levelled, and TikToks of neighbourhoods razed. They then saw news headlines reprint Israeli talking points and news anchors sanitize[1] events in antiseptic language about death tolls[2] and "collateral damage."[3]

Talia, a 22-year-old in Vancouver, called it a "radical shift" in her relationship with news. She pointed to how Western outlets described some deaths as "retaliatory" or due to "natural causes," while others were labelled "massacres."[4] "It's like they're trying to tell me what I should care about," she said. The Incubator for Media Education and Development (iMEdD)[5] and the Scottish news site the *National*[6] have published studies on the killed-vs-died reporting style, which underline how Palestinian deaths are often reported using a passive voice, obscuring the perpetrator.

This disconnect cemented something deeper: the belief that legacy media are not just biased, but complicit in Palestinian suffering. The erosion of trust is reflected in broader trends: the 2025 Digital News Report[7] found that only 37 per cent of English news consumers in Canada say they trust the news, down from 47 per cent four years earlier.

Inside the Newsroom Gag Order

For the past 22 months (and long before October 7, 2023), newsrooms have fed this alienation. Coverage has conflated Palestine with Islam, muddled criticism of the Israeli government with antisemitism, and regurgitated IDF/Hasbara talking points. Palestinian voices have been absent from news coverage or relegated to "both-sides" panels that require them to denounce Hamas. Reporting routinely leans on official Israeli statements[8] while casting doubt on Palestinian sources (i.e., a pattern of referring to Gaza's "Hamas-run" Health Ministry, whose figures have been deemed reliable by sources including *The Lancet* health journal).[9] The billionaire-funded lobby group, HonestReporting Canada (HRC),[10] has mounted organized campaigns to police and control coverage; strong-arming newsrooms across the country into redactions and retractions. Journalists who challenge these framings have faced consequences. It's a common story in Canadian newsrooms.

Colleagues across the country have faced similar silencing and erasure in their attempts to petition their newsrooms for representative coverage. In May 2021, after one of the deadliest attacks on Gaza, hundreds of journalists signed an open letter to Canadian newsrooms calling for fairer and more balanced coverage.[11] Within days, the *Intercept* reported "at least three people were completely taken off coverage of the region,"[12] and two CBC journalists told *Vice News* they'd been barred from covering the region.[13]

Since Oct. 7, the stories from inside the newsroom kept mounting. In my essay, "Why I Left CTV News: The Fight for Press Freedom in Canada,"[14] I recount how my own piece on the Wet'suwet'en protests was quietly removed from the network's website following a harassment campaign conducted by HonestReporting Canada. Molly Schumann penned a scathing expose[15] on how CBC has whitewashes Israel's crimes; *The Breach* revealed a CTV policy forbidding its journalists from using the word

Palestine on air;[16] journalism professor Shenaz Kermalli has chronicled systemic suppression of Palestinian-focused reporting.[17] There have been so many accounts of internal resistance; *The Breach* compiled them into an anthology titled, *When Genocide Wasn't News* (including my essay on my experience with CTV).[18]

Together, these stories suggest the gulf between journalists and their own institutions is as much a part of the trust crisis as the content viewers see on screen. One CBC journalist told me none of the recent famine-focused coverage comes from a place of concern for human life. "I see journalists and organizations as either trying to save face because they know they didn't cover this story properly for the past 78 years, or they see the starvation angle as a 'safe' way to cover Palestine without explicitly blaming Israel for it." By foregrounding starvation—which can be framed as a tragic by-product of war (unlike bombing campaigns or forced displacement)—media organizations are able to acknowledge suffering while avoiding explicit criticism of the Israeli government.

A Mic for Netanyahu

The limits of this approach were on display August 10, 2025, as the flurry of famine-focused coverage came to a halt. Instead, networks broadcast Israeli prime minister Benjamin Netanyahu's press conference live, uninterrupted, as he blamed Gazans' deaths on Hamas (not his own military) and pledged to "finish the job"[19] and take over Gaza. Canadian headlines simply reiterated his pledge to expand Israel's offensive.[20] They largely excluded any Palestinian perspective.

Hours later, Israel targeted a tent of the last remaining *Al Jazeera* reporters in Gaza, killing six journalists, including Anas al-Sharif, the most prominent correspondent in the region.[21] Israeli officials accused him of heading a Hamas cell but have provided no proof, no evidence. A UN special rapporteur and press freedom group say the claims are unsubstantiated, but that didn't stop the *National Post*[22] from running with Israel's story.

According to the United Nations human rights office, the toll of murdered journalists since Oct. 7 is 247 as of the end of August, 2025.[23] In another stark example of media complicity, a report by *The Maple*[24] reveals that CBC acquiesced to an Israeli censorship order to not record or broadcast images of a recent aid drop over Gaza. This is the backdrop against which any talk of a "shift" in coverage must be judged.

The humanitarian framing also dovetails with political messaging. On July 21, Canada joined France and the UK in a joint statement that condemned Israel's "dangerous" aid distribution system and said the war in Gaza "must end now," yet avoided using the word genocide or calling for sanctions.[25] Days later, Prime Minister Mark Carney accused Israel of violating international law by denying humanitarian aid.[26] Ottawa has hinted it will recognize a Palestinian state[27] but only after elections are held, even though Gaza is largely destroyed and 147 of the UN's 193 member states already recognize Palestine as sovereign. Framing the crisis as a matter of "aid delivery" allows governments to scold Israel while keeping diplomatic levers, and use recognition of a Palestinian state as bargaining chips.

This isn't simply an argument about adjectives. Language shapes reality. When the media describes a siege as a "blockade" or a massacre as a "toll," it erases agency and dulls outrage. As long as journalists hesitate to name starvation and mass killing as genocide, they shield those in power from accountability. That is not neutrality; it is complicity.

When mainstream coverage fails, audiences turn elsewhere. My research participants described scrolling TikTok, Instagram, and citizen-journalism feeds—unfiltered, raw, decentralized, and often unvetted. This comes with pitfalls: propaganda, misinformation, and news burnout. But it's the devil they choose. "At least on social media, I feel like I have a choice in what I see," said 24-year-old Maria. Most participants relied on accounts with unabashed viewpoints. "At least they're honest about where they're coming from," said 24-year-old Omar.

When young Canadians find more honesty in influencers' admitted biases than in a newsroom's claims of objectivity, it becomes clear that the erosion of trust in journalism isn't about isolated errors. It's about newsrooms clinging to a hollow notion of neutrality.

Audiences see the patterns: who is interviewed and who isn't, which words are chosen, whose humanity is recognized. If journalists want to rebuild trust, the solution isn't to retreat into false "balance" or further police their language. It is to show that journalism can be a force for justice. That means centring underrepresented voices, reporting facts even when they implicate our allies, and resisting coordinated campaigns to rewrite the narrative. It also means readers and viewers must hold media institutions to account: support outlets that practice rigorous and transparent reporting; call out euphemisms that whitewash atrocities; demand accountability from our public broadcaster; and use your platforms to amplify those on the ground.

Journalism matters because words have power. Let's use them honestly. Let's call starvation a war crime, displacement ethnic cleansing, and mass killing genocide when the evidence supports it.[28] Name complicity when governments hedge their statements and delay recognition while civilians starve. A free press must be willing to confront power, not simply echo it. Only then can legacy media begin to rebuild trust with a generation that has seen too much to accept euphemism over truth.

Notes

1. Jason Toney, "National Post quietly rewrote wire stories to push pro-Israel narrative, analysis finds," *The Breach*, 10 June 2025.
2. Jason Toney, "Toronto Star Death Toll Language Biased and Data Confirms It," The Media Accountability Project, 9 May 2024.
3. Chris Brown, "Will the missile attack that killed aid workers change Israeli minds about the Gaza war?" *CBC News*, 3 April 2024.
4. Sean Seddon, Joshua Cheetham, Benedict Garman, "Supernova festival: How massacre unfolded from verified video and social media," *BBC News*, 10 October 2023.
5. "Dead versus Killed: A Closer Look at the Media Bias in Reporting Israel-Palestine Conflict," *The Wire*, 4 December 2023.
6. Xander Elliards, "Study shows BBC bias in reporting on Palestinian and Israeli deaths," *The National-Scot*, 9 January 2024.
7. Nic Newman, et al, Reuters Institute Digital News Report 2025, Reuters Institute for the Study of Journalism.
8. "Israel uncovers major Hamas command centre in Gaza City as ceasefire talks gain momentum," *CTV News*, 20 December 2023.
9. Benjamin Q. Huyṅh, et al, "No evidence of inflated mortality reporting from the Gaza Ministry of Health," *The Lancet*, Volume 403, Issue 10421, P23-24, 6 January 2024.
10. See Appendix, HonestReporting Canada.

11. "Canadians call for fairness, impartiality, and integrity on Palestine," Open Letter to CBC, from CBC Palestine, Canadians for Peace and Justice in the Middle East, the Coalition of Canadian Palestinian Organizations, July 2021.
12. Akela Lacy, "Canadian journalists fear retaliation for criticizing coverage of Israeli attacks on Gaza," *The Intercept*, 20 May 2021.
13. Manisha Krishnan, "CBC Journalists Told They Can't Cover Israel-Palestine After Demanding Fairer Coverage," *Vice News*, 21 May 2021.
14. Iman Kassam, "Why I Left CTV News: The Fight for Press Freedom in Canada," *The Rover*, 24 October 2024.
15. Molly Schumann, "CBC has whitewashed Israel's crimes in Gaza. I saw it first hand," *The Breach*, 16 May 2024.
16. Emma Paling, "CTV forbids use of 'Palestine,' suppresses critical stories about Israel," *The Breach*, 22 November 2023.
17. Shenaz Kermalli, "Canadian newsrooms are stifling Palestinian perspectives," *J-Source*, 23 December 2023.
18. Martin Lukacs, editor. *When Genocide Wasn't News*. Montreal, Breach Books, 2025.
19. "Netanyahu lashes out at 'global campaign of lies' as widespread criticism over Gaza mounts," *CBC News*, 10 August 2025.
20. "Netanyahu defends Gaza plan condemned at home and abroad," *Calgary Herald*, 10 August 2025.
21. "Israel kills Al Jazeera journalists in targeted Gaza City airstrike," Committee to Protect Journalists, 13 August 2025.
22. "Israeli strike in Gaza slays Anas al-Sharif, who Israel says posed as an 'Al Jazeera' journalist while directing rocket attacks for Hamas," *National Post*, 11 August 2025.
23. "Killing of journalists in Gaza hospital attack 'should shock the world': UN rights office," *UN News*, 26 August 2025.
24. Alex Cosh, "CBC Agreed to Follow Israeli Censorship Order on Gaza Aid Drop Flight," *The Maple*, 12 August 2025.
25. Joint statement on behalf of 26 partners on the Occupied Palestinian Territories. Global Affairs Canada, Government of Canada, 21 July 2025.
26. Holly Cabrera, "Carney calls Israel denying humanitarian aid in Gaza 'violation of international law'," *CBC News*, 24 July 2025.
27. Statement by Prime Minister Carney on Canada's recognition of a Palestinian state. Prime Minister of Canada, 30 July 2025.
28. "As mass starvation spreads across Gaza, our colleagues and those we serve are wasting away." Statement, Oxfam Canada, 23 July 2025.

CHAPTER 10

Why Don't We Tell the Truth?

Samira Mohyeddin

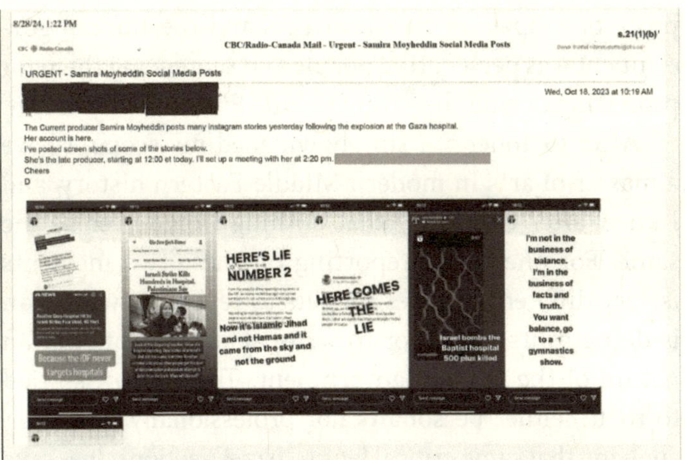

8/28/24, 1:22 PM

s.21(1)(b)'

CBC/Radio-Canada Mail - Urgent - Samira Moyheddin Social Media Posts

URGENT - Samira Moyheddin Social Media Posts

Wed, Oct 18, 2023 at 10:19 AM

The Current producer Samira Moyheddin posts many instagram stories yesterday following the explosion at the Gaza hospital.
Her account is here.
I've posted screen shots of some of the stories below.
She's the late producer, starting at 12:00 et today. I'll set up a meeting with her at 2:20 pm.
Cheers
D

Mohyeddin submitted a Freedom of Information Act request to the CBC for all emails and Google messages that included the words "Samira" or "Mohyeddin" and/or "Gaza" "Palestine" or "Israel" from September 7, 2023 to August 18, 2024. In October 2023, she received a 794-page document that included this exchange between CBC managers. In November 2023, after a feeling of being "institutionally hunted," she resigned from the CBC.

LEILA MARSHY: Prior to October 7, 2023, I was following your online activity about Iran, specifically the Woman, Life, Freedom movement. You provided an enormous amount of information and kept the issue alive and urgent for many in Canada and elsewhere. After October 7 you pivoted to Palestine. Can you talk a little bit about why you did that, and whether the reaction/backlash has been different regarding your Palestine advocacy vs the Iran advocacy?
First and foremost, I am a journalist. I follow the story. In 2023, the story for me was Iran because there were protests happening on the streets and the Iranian government was persecuting people and sentencing them for protesting during the Woman, Life, Freedom movement.

After October 7, I simply widened my scope. I have a master of arts in modern Middle Eastern history, and I knew after October 7 that nothing would ever be the same. For one thing, reporting on these two incidents is very different. It takes no guts to report on what Iran is doing to its people or to write about the totalitarian nature of the Iranian government. There's no risk tied to that; neither personally nor professionally. However, applying that same critical lens to Israel's actions does take journalistic guts. You have to be prepared for attacks on your credibility, your livelihood, and in the case of almost 250 Palestinian journalists, your life.

Of all the mainstream Canadian journalists and media people who have been politically outspoken this past year, you probably have one of the highest profiles. Why do you think journalists have otherwise been mostly silent and/or exceedingly careful? Do you think

journalists are feeling censored—or do they just not care? Will this affect your career going forward?
Over the past year and a half, we watched broadcasters and producers either resign or be forced off the air and it's not just one or two. I don't think it's a matter of journalists "feeling" censored; we know we are censored, it's not a feeling. Censorship takes many forms. Self-censorship is most prevalent around this issue because it gets exhausting to always come up against the same arguments when pitching stories on Palestine and Israel. So, you don't pitch.

Why don't we tell the truth? That's a great question. The other question is why do we sacrifice the truth at the altar of so-called objectivity or balance? Palestine has been officially, legally, and physically occupied and under military rule since 1967, not to mention it was violently partitioned in 1948. Palestinians live under a brutal military occupation, and at best they are treated as second-class citizens even within Israel. This is an undeniable verifiable truth; it is systemic and written into the laws of the state of Israel. Despite this, you will hear some journalists use terms like "disputed territories," or they ignore the fact that Israel abducts 400 to 600 Palestinian children per year and tries them in military courts—the only country in the world to do this. These children are often held for long periods without charge.

The core of the problem in the mainstream media is that we look at Gaza as a humanitarian issue. If only they had more money. If only we could get more food or aid to them. It's never looked at as a political problem, which is exactly what it is. Israel is an occupying state, specifically one that shirks its responsibilities under international law.

That should not be a radical statement to make. It should also not be controversial.

This dissonance has affected my career. For starters, what has happened since October 7, 2023, is that my eyes have really widened. You know when you go to an eye exam and they put drops in your eyes and things become too clear, that's what Palestine has done to my eyesight. Once you start to tell the truth of what is going on in Palestine and you look at Israel's actions truthfully and you don't obfuscate and you use the right words to describe occupation and apartheid, you can't go back into the mainstream media. They see you as a live wire and as a liability for their advertisers and stakeholders. That's the point at which I decided to leave mainstream media, particularly CBC. I know the politics and the history of this occupation too well to pretend, and I was being treated as if my knowledge was not an asset but a liability for my employer. I just didn't want to remain somewhere where that was the case.

I would argue that media outlets and managers have doubled down on pushing a pro-Israeli narrative. This despite the maniacal genocide we have watched unfold on our phones and despite every single human rights organization and the highest court in the world calling it a genocide. They have doubled down on not providing history and context. They have doubled down on showing Palestine and Palestinians as being a purely humanitarian issue with little focus on Israel's apartheid system and structure.

At one point you posted: "In all my 15 years of journalism and broadcasting, I have never ever been so threat-

ened or had my sexuality or gender weaponized against me. Supporters of Israeli policy are truly some of the most vile and violent people I have ever encountered." Can you speak about what you have experienced?
Speaking the truth about Palestine has very real consequences. I've had Canadian members of parliament target and harass me online. I've also had people harass me in the streets, calling me antisemitic, threatening me with gender-based violence, or pummelling me with homophobic slurs. There is no shortage of the types of harassment that I have received since covering and being vocal about Gaza.

I'll give you other examples. I had gone to cover a protest at the University of Toronto campus on October 21, 2024. A Columbia University professor, Shai Davidai, had come to the university with a group of Zionist protesters to hold an "antisemitism rally." While I was covering the protest, homophobic slurs were levelled at me by a woman who used to be a columnist for a major newspaper here in Canada. I hadn't been called a dyke since high school, not in a derogatory way, and all I kept thinking was these people are supposed to be the progressive ones. You know, as a queer journalist I'm constantly told that if I went to Gaza they would throw me off a roof; my sexuality is weaponized against my humanity.

What's also interesting about this is that I'm just supposed to just take it. I'm supposed to think, "oh well, this is part of the job." But this was never part of my job. I never signed up for this. I never signed up for my family's restaurant windows to be smashed in. I've covered dozens of conflicts, wars, and even other genocides, but I've never been threatened in this way ever. So that tells me something.

That tells me that there is something systemic at play and nefarious and organized, and that the truth is a threat.

While Canada does not have a version of AIPAC operating in this country, we are vulnerable to lobby pressure, and our government is extremely reluctant to do anything but parrot American talking points in support of Israel. Why is that so? Do you see any breaks in this unwavering support for Israel? Prime Minister Chrétien resisted the push to invade Iraq in 2003 and our intelligence was vocal about the lack of evidence for a WMD program—why can't the Trudeau and now Carney governments be similarly independent in their approach? Well, Trudeau did deviate slightly from America in that he said he would abide by Canada's obligations as a signatory to the ICC. Meaning, Netanyahu and Gallant would be arrested if they come to Canada. And now Carney is making statements that are vague enough to appear controversial to Zionists.

But Iraq was Iraq and this is Israel. This is the "Palestine exception" on full display. Canada is duplicitous when it comes to Palestine. We have consistently voted against recognizing Palestine as a state in the United Nations, and we have refused to condemn Israeli settlements. How can you say that you are working towards a two-state solution when you don't even recognize the other state? Harper firmly embraced a pro-Israel position, while Trudeau maybe was not so firm, but he parroted most American talking points. We'll see with Carney.

Meanwhile, Canada has adopted one of the most controversial and contested definitions of antisemitism, that of the International Holocaust Remembrance Alliance

(IHRA).[1] Jewish Holocaust studies professors and genocide studies professors have all noted that this is a dangerous definition, as it conflates critiques of Israel and Israeli policy with antisemitism.

While we may not have organizations like AIPAC in this country that go all out to determine electoral victories in the United States, we do have such entities as B'nai Brith and the CIJA (Centre for Israel and Jewish Affairs).[2] They are just as effective in promulgating Israel's talking points in Canada and putting pressure on Canadian politicians to support Israel at every turn. Numerous Canadian politicians have gone on fully paid trips to Israel since October 7, for example, to take part in Israeli propaganda junkets.

Has Canadian media risen to the task of covering this conflict? Has your assessment of the Canadian media landscape changed or evolved since October 7?

Canadian media capital M, no. Specific Canadian journalists, absolutely. My assessment of the media landscape hasn't changed. I also differ with some in terms of asking if media has risen to the occasion because I would argue that media outlets and managers have actually doubled down on pushing a pro-Israeli narrative. This is despite the maniacal genocide we have watched unfold on our phones and despite every single human rights organization and the highest court in the world calling it a genocide. They have doubled down on not providing history and context. They have doubled down on showing Palestine and Palestinians as being a purely humanitarian issue with little focus on Israel's apartheid system and structure.

One of the things that has left an indelible mark on me since October 7, other than the egregious impunity with which Israel has exacted this genocide, was a very specific incident that looks at Canada's footprint in Gaza and Israel's actions on the ground and the media response to it. We are going to kill three birds with one incident.

On July 26, 2024, Israeli soldiers mined and blew up the solar-powered water treatment plant in Rafah. This plant served nearly a hundred thousand people with fresh water. It had been built and paid for 25 years ago by CIDA (Canadian International Development Agency) and was known as the "Canada Well." I put the news of its destruction on my page on X and waited. I waited to see how long it would take for the Canadian media to cover it. And I waited and waited. Normally, we would have been all over this story. Finding the engineers who worked on it. Talking to government officials. Discussing its critical usefulness, and so on.

It took five days for an article to come out. CBC covered it but turned it into a story about Ahmed Hussen, Minister of International Development, saying he would run for office again and recommitting to freezing Canadian funding to UNRWA.

No mention of how even before October 7, 2023, Palestinians were systematically deprived of water in Gaza and had already been enduring a water crisis because of the siege. No mention that on October 9, 2023, Defense Minister Yoav Gallant had given a directive in saying all water would be cut off. No mention that the soldier who filmed himself blowing up the water plant said he did it "in honour of Shabbat." Instead, the article's main focus was that Canada had asked Israel to investigate.

In what world do we ask the criminal to investigate themselves? In what world do journalists not follow patterns or see connections? Not to mention, it has been over a year since Canada put that request in; has there been any follow-up to see what happened? Anything in the media?

This is what I mean when I say things have not only not changed; in fact, they've gotten worse. The divide between government, the enabling media, and the people is widening. The majority of people have become wise to Israel's criminality, the occupation and its policies of apartheid. They expect their government to sanction or isolate or condemn Israel, yet they see the opposite. Worse, in the case of some countries, such as Germany and the United States, they are seeing their tax dollars go to arming Israel.

You began *On the Line* in August 2024, an independent podcast where you speak to a wide variety of media, academic, and arts guests about Palestine and Iran. This analysis and coverage are almost entirely absent from mainstream media. What do you make of that?
Audiences are hungry for context and history and root causes. They want to be able to make sense of what they see happening in their world. I like making those connections and providing a throughline. You are not going to hear a lot of "balanced" journalism on my program. I believe in truth with a capital T, not duelling narratives given equal time. There are facts and I present them as such. My tagline for the podcast is "Bringing you the voices you most need to hear from, now."

Many people are pushed to the fringes and have their voices marginalized because they don't obfuscate about what Israel does to the Palestinians, and they have shown exemplary courage over the past year by standing up and speaking out. I want to highlight those people. I want to use my platform to uplift the people who are doing the important work on the ground and beyond. I want them to become household names because courage is infectious.

All dictators fall; whether in Iran or Israel. Israel's systemic subjugation of Palestinians will come to an end eventually. How many Gazan civilians and Israeli citizens will die before that happens is entirely up to Israel.

Incredibly, the UN Special Rapporteur on Palestine was snubbed by the Canadian government when she visited in November 2023. How serious was this snub, and what does it say about the Canadian government?
I think it's important to point out that she wasn't merely snubbed. There was a concerted effort by Zionist organizations in Canada to vilify her and they demanded that government officials not meet with her while she was here.

What's also interesting is that while they didn't meet with Francesca Albanese, the Foreign Affairs committee heard from former Israeli spokesperson Elon Levy about why Canada should not recognize Palestine as a state. So, they took the time to meet with Elon Levy, a man who was fired from his position as Israeli spokesperson for lying, but they didn't meet with the United Nations Special Rapporteur. This speaks volumes about Canada and its priorities when it comes to this issue.

In the early months of this conflict, it felt like the world was finally catching up to the plight of the Palestinians and that there might be consensus that the Israeli state was an oppressor. But the pushback to this—media,

government, etc.—has been ferocious. Do you have any predictions about where we might be a year from now? This is a difficult question because we are currently in the tsunami of a Trump administration. Every day is exhausting. Every day a new set of absurd executive orders. We realized quickly who the enemies are for the new America: LGBTQ people, migrants, women, and anything to do with diversity, equity, or inclusion. We are in a whirlwind of an administration that is continuing the process of breaking down all the institutions that were formed by the international community, a process Israel began on October 7, 2023. The attacks on the United Nations, for example, both rhetorical and physical, are unprecedented.

As cynical as we would like to be about these institutions, they are all we have and we need to build them up rather than attack them. I don't know what is to come but I am afraid that it will only get worse. I see a complete annexation of the occupied West Bank and further attacks against NGOs and human rights organizations. Israel's Knesset passed a bill this year putting an 80 per cent tax on foreign government donations to Israeli and Palestinian civil society organisations. These are the groups that document Israel's apartheid and these are the organizations that put their bodies on the line between rabid settlers and soldiers in the occupied West Bank. What this law does effectively is kill international solidarity with the Palestinians and those Israeli organizations working for liberation for all.

Notes

1. See Appendix, IHRA Working Definition of Antisemitism.
2. See Appendix, Political Lobbying.

CHAPTER 11

Floods Come in Waves

Nora Loreto

1

It's October 7, 2023; a day that changed media in Canada. Virtually overnight, silent gatekeepers dropped the portcullis, locked up access tight, made sure that no one could accidentally be allowed to say what was plain truth to anyone paying attention.

I have always had a difficult time with the gatekeepers. Since I had been blacklisted by most mainstream media outlets in 2018, a freeze had been thawing. The only problem? That thaw coincided with an unprecedented loss of media jobs.

Newspapers became thinner. Magazines printed less often. Online publications accepted fewer and fewer articles. And in the first few weeks after the Oct. 7 attacks, media didn't want to hear from anyone who wanted to say the obvious: that if you create a pressure cooker by dehumanizing people, violating and controlling them for generations, they will fight back.

There should have been enough space in this conversation to talk about all the violence towards every victim, about the loved ones who were captured on Oct. 7 as well as the loved ones who had been captured long before that. But the conversation itself was impossible. No mainstream outlet would touch it, just like they barely touched the most important story: that Israel retaliated against Hamas by reigning hell down upon Gaza, with a ferocity and precision that has never before been seen in modern warfare.

Canadian media could not countenance any deviation from the official line: Israel was doing self defense. Israel was doing proportionality. Israel was defending her honour. To challenge any of this was to put one's career on the line. But I didn't think twice about the decisions I made. I would lose tens of thousands of dollars in work. For example, despite my being a regular, *Canadaland* ghosted me (fine, the feeling was mutual). I had fewer magazine opportunities than I had had in years.

At least, I still had the CBC and a Sunday morning panel where average people talked about politics or culture. Every few weeks, I was on as an average person. We were writers and artists, business people and professors—not politicos or flaks. We were expected to talk about ordinary though pressing subjects. But each week following Oct. 7, 2023, the show dodged the most pressing subject in the world. There was no way on earth to stop one of us from talking about what we saw happening in Gaza.

Sometime between Christmas and New Year's, we average people got an email from our producer who said that despite the segment's popularity, we were being swept out as part of the latest round of funding cuts to the public broadcaster. Given that the segment was not all that expensive (they paid us appearance fees, not salaries), and given that the segment was popular, I wondered— how much did this decision have to do with Oct. 7? It's not a stretch to imagine that they pre-emptively cancelled the segment out of fear that one of us would be honest on air. And that none of us would defend Israel's actions.

I haven't worked for CBC since.

2

It's April, 2024. I receive an email about annual Passover celebrations. I RSVP: two adults, two kids.

I'm not Jewish and my partner is a staunch atheist. But when we lived in Toronto, we always attended a Passover seder at his aunt and uncle's house. It was casual and I looked forward to seeing the full moon over the small cul-de-sac that his family lived on in Thornhill each spring.

When we moved to Quebec City, we felt it important to keep our kids' connection to their Jewish side so that they had a base as adults to move closer to it if they chose. Quebec City's Jewish community is tiny. Minuscule. Its synagogue is in a 60s modern house in an inner suburb. More than one hundred years of Jewish history is crammed into what is a living room in the identical house beside.

Gradually, we got more involved, participating in Purim, marking Rosh Hashanah. The tiny community filled the same role for most of the people who participated there; events and meals that would normally be celebrated with family and friends were celebrated together because family and friends were so far away.

But it was April 2024, and things were different. When I RSVP'd for Passover, rather than receiving a confirmation,

I was told that my family would not be allowed to participate in the seder this year. Unnamed members of the synagogue's executive opposed my partner's activism in Independent Jewish Voices. They would be made uncomfortable if we were present. They couldn't take the risk that perhaps Israel would come up in conversation (not from us—we knew who we could talk politics with and who we could not) and worse, perhaps there'd be people present who agreed that Israel was committing a genocide.

We didn't go. Luckily, I had ordered everything in advance so we could have a seder at home (because you cannot buy matzos in Quebec City), something that we started to do in 2020. This year, to make the necessary purchases, we will buy through Amazon for the first time in my life.

My children's Jewish lineage passes up through their grandfather, whose family was mostly killed in the Holocaust. His parents emigrated after the war and made a life in Canada that they probably couldn't have imagined being possible while they were interned in Uzbekistan and Siberia by the Russian Army.

The irony, then, that the familial connections to Judaism might be stamped out by a couple of unnamed members of a tiny synagogue executive.

It's Quebec City. There are no other options for us to try and maintain that connection. So my kids will have to figure it out on their own as adults, knowing that a stranger's fidelity to a foreign land was so strong, that my kids were not allowed to simply celebrate the story of Passover.

We aren't the only family who no longer comes out to the synagogue because of this.

3

It's October 7, 2024. One year has passed since the Earth opened up, bared its teeth, and started swallowing people whole in Gaza. One year, literally countless dead (because it is difficult to count the dead), countless injured, families obliterated, civil infrastructure destroyed, land cratered and poisoned. Gaza partitioned between the north and the south.

No, that isn't right. The Earth didn't open up on its own. Israel responded to a Hamas-led offensive with ferocity. With unflinching violence and rage; the kind of rage of an occupier who sees the occupied walk across his front lawn, multiplied by one billion. One year has passed since October 7, 2023, and it feels like everything has changed. It has, yet nothing has stopped.

As a writer, it is impossible for me to not mark this one-year anniversary. I desperately need to write something. But where? Who will publish me? In the past year, my options to publish have narrowed to the narrowest they have ever been. I know that few magazines are going to publish a retrospective sympathetic to Gaza. Certainly no newspaper. The blogs are in short supply. Besides, there are better people than me to write about this.

Writing a short-form piece feels impossible but I am working through my first magazine feature since summer 2023. It's about Gaza, but in its specifics: how experts count the dead during a period of war. Gaza. The war against ISIS in Iraq and Syria. Rwanda. The editors and I work hard to make sure that the piece is airtight. Bulletproof against the Zionists who are organising to stop people like me from ever being hired again; the ones who get their hands on the article before it's published and literally write a missive about why no one should ever hire me. I'm proud of the piece, but I have no idea that in five months an editor will change one of my sentences and replace the word *attack* with the word *massacre*. "Hamas-led massacre" becomes how I describe what happened on October 7, 2023, using numbers provided by Israel that we will later learn are false.

I, as in my name is on the piece but not *I* as in actually me.

But this won't happen until 2025. It's still October 7, 2024 and while writing a feature takes months, I need to find somewhere that will publish me, today. And so, I take refuge in a sanctuary that I've set up to make sure I can always go somewhere. My own lean-to in the forest. Walk past buildings and homes that are shabby, though warm, and crawl into the one place that I don't have to worry about the reaction I'll get from Zionists for daring to criticize their Zionism: my little blog.

I write,

> *We pray that the price of oil goes up. We pray for the largest US military staging area outside of United States territory. We pray to keep the spoils of war. We pray for the profits made when a child is blown into 244 little pieces, pieces that her father imagines picking up and putting back together so that he can hold his girl whole one last time.*
>
> *The profits made when the death toll goes up, when the hospital reaches five times its capacity. When the Blessed President Joe Biden discusses bombing Iranian oil fields.*

In the name of The Profits, and of the land and of manifest destiny. We clasp our hands and beg to the Holy Spirit to make all of this stop. Perhaps violent intercession is all we can hope for. Of Netanyahu hanging upside down. Of average Israelis storming the Knesset and forcing the government out. Of Iran destroying every Israeli runway that has the capacity to receive more weapons.

We clasp the hands of our comrades and our friends. We thread our fingers in between the fingers of our children and thank God that by a stroke of cosmic luck, we were not born there. By a stroke of cosmic luck, we were born somewhere that keeps its hands clean while it only quietly encourages the violence to continue. The luck of living on the side of the perpetrator.

Knowing that I could never write this anywhere else.

4

It's March, 2025. Students are being disappeared from the streets of American campuses. One has fled to Toronto. There are spurious accusations, including sympathy and support for Hamas. If you don't want to be deported, you should deport yourself voluntarily, the White House says.

I've been censored and silenced before, and while we have yet to set up a Guantanamo Bay or El Salvadoran detention centre for Canadians, we are still paying a price for calling what Israel is doing a genocide. Challenging Zionism is going to result in professional repercussions. When colonialism is constructed on top of a lie, that lie must be maintained at all costs. For now, that lie remains indestructible. For now. All that being said, it's impossible to watch what is happening in the United States and feel bad about any professional repercussions that I've experienced. It's unthinkable to watch life in Gaza and feel bad about any professional repercussions that I've experienced.

But what I do despair over is the lack of space to even talk about this. For now there is no opportunity to have a debate about power and control, about occupiers and their rotten governments. For now, there can be no space to talk about Gaza, about Palestinians, in all the diversity and complexity that humanity requires. We cannot do this because Palestinians cannot be humanized, because antisemitism.

It remains difficult to plainly say what is obviously true: Israel targets hospitals. Israel targets civilians. Israel uses human shields and tortures detainees. Amid the news of another family wiped out, it is still costly to state what is obviously true: Israel wants Gaza gone and they are working to achieve this.

You can try to say these things, but how? Those who speak out have lost our platforms and our tribunes. No one calls us for analysis. And increasingly, mass platforms have lost their audiences too. Average people don't want to be called antisemitic for saying that Israel should stop bombing hospitals or schools or children. Average people don't want their tax dollars used to supply weapons to Israel or to purchase weapons from Israel. Average people still believe that Palestinians are inexplicably violent and that Israel must be protected.

All because the lie that underpins colonization must be maintained. Shield politicians from these questions. Hide public opinion. Above all else, do not give anyone who might state these things a spot on live television where they could go off on a hot mic. If the average Canadian heard someone speak the truth, it could spark a revolution.

Colonies stick together and Canada and Israel are close friends. When will the flood happen? When will the consensus be broken? When will popular pressure and support for justice be strong enough that Canada's ruling class cannot ignore it?

That's the most important part of this story: The people who hold power in this country have thin mandates and little popular support. They know how fragile their positions are. If a crack in their hold on power appears, it will not be able to withstand the rush of water that will flow through it, breaking apart the consensus that they work so hard to maintain. And then? I hope that someday, we'll know what happens then. Because one thing is certain: with justice on our side, and hard work, that someday isn't theoretical; it's simply one of the days after tomorrow.

5

It's warmish. An early spring day in Edmonton. I receive a text that says: *They're out! They're out!* My friend, trapped in Canada while his family is in Gaza, tells me that we did it. Our Hail-Mary shot worked. Timing and luck conspired and his wife and children managed to leave Gaza.

For the timing, we can thank the intergenerational memory of the impact of fleeing war and the trauma that comes alongside it. My partner makes the decision. *If my family had waited another week to escape Poland, they would have been dead. They had a choice to leave with the Russians or wait for the Nazis. The town was divided. People made different decisions and my family managed to make the right one. We have to move when we can.*

And so, after months of a dozen or more people working behind the scenes, doing what was possible to try and bring our friend's family to Canada through official programs, with official papers and official relations with officials in official places, we gather the money and pay for their exit. Within eight days, they're safe in Egypt.

A week later, Israel closes the Rafah border crossing, making such timing and luck impossible for anyone else. They got out but everyone else is trapped. What was once referred to as the world's largest open-air prison grinds to become the world's largest death camp. You can run from the bombs but, at some point, you might find yourself running out of time.

My friend is an expert in civil infrastructure. When he first left Gaza for a short academic appointment in Canada, he didn't expect that he would be stuck here. The systems upon which his academic study and expertise are based are being blown up and sabotaged by the Israeli military.

His work will never be the same. He isn't blacklisted or quietly managed out of positions. Not fired for wearing a pin representing Palestine or targeted by an online mob until his employer relents and fires him. His career, like the careers of his fellow Gazans, has simply been destroyed. Today, he and his wife navigate this new country and new life, while their children learn French in their local neighbourhood school.

Silence will not save us. All we have is solidarity, and the good news is that we have solidarity in abundance.

PART THREE

NO IVORY TOWER

Photo: Safa Chebbi

CHAPTER 12

Uncompromising Solidarity: Struggling for Political Memory

Safa Chebbi

The emergence of university encampments in solidarity with Palestine in spring 2024 marked a turning point in Montreal's activist landscape. Led primarily by students, they transformed how we become involved, make political alliances, and practice solidarity in response to the escalating genocide in Gaza. They embodied a logic of deliberate confrontation, affirming the centrality of the anti-colonial struggle and challenging existing normative frameworks.

The student group Solidarity for Palestinian Human Rights (SPHR-SDHPP), present on several campuses, played a pivotal role. With branches at McGill, Concordia, Université du Québec à Montréal (UQAM), and the Université de Montréal (UdeM), it coordinated targeted actions against the institutions' ties to the Zionist entity, while adapting the modes of mobilization to contexts specific to each campus.

The establishment of the first encampment at McGill on April 27, 2024, was a pivotal moment. More than an act of protest, the encampment opened a physical space for political experimentation, bringing together activists with diverse backgrounds, white and non-white, French-speaking and English-speaking. It was more radical than previous forms of mobilization and filled a strategic void left by more than seven months of genocide, channeling popular anger and responding to the inability of historical structures to rise to the challenge. It also helped overcome the waning momentum of a mobilization that had until then been punctuated by weekly demonstrations and a few scattered direct actions.

Within two weeks, approximately ten encampments sprang up across Canada, marking an unprecedented acceleration of mobilization and a reappropriation of campuses as spaces for political expression. These encampments included: University of Alberta; University of British Columbia, Vancouver Campus; University of Ottawa; University of Toronto; University of Calgary and more.

UQAM students, who were at the McGill encampment from day one, created a space to bring together the French-speaking community thanks to the involvement of SDHPP-UQAM, which also played a key role in organizing the camp's logistics and overall vitality. After two weeks, the UQAM students launched their own camp on May 12, expanding the free zones across Tiohtià:ke (Montreal) and consolidating the reach of the engagement across the island.

Dubbed "Université Populaire Al-Aqsa (Al-Aqsa People's University)," this encampment aimed to multiply spaces for struggle while highlighting the complicity of French-language institutions, often absent from public debate, and confronting them with their own responsibilities. Drawing inspiration from the history of social and political struggles at UQAM, this encampment also brought together students from the UdeM and French-language CEGEPs (junior colleges), actively involving them in the mobilization.

Resistance vs Repression

The proliferation of encampments was inevitably accompanied by multifaceted institutional repression that intensified as the mobilization grew in scale. At McGill, for example, the administration immediately declared the encampment illegal and launched a series of legal proceedings with the goal of terminating it. In addition, police surveillance was continually reinforced and included regular patrols around the encampment, sparking moments of tension and intimidation.

Repression escalated constantly and reached a peak on June 6, 2024, when the Montreal police riot squad brutally intervened. During that raid, the police used tear gas and batons, arresting 13 people, several of whom were injured. That intervention, which received significant media coverage, aimed to break the encampment's momentum and deter further mobilization.

Repression was not only physical. A symbolic and media offensive was deployed to destabilize supporters and marginalize the participants, and neutralize any form of support for the pro-Palestine movement within the university itself. Classic accusations of antisemitism were leveled at activists, aimed at tarnishing the encampment's image. Pressure was exerted on professors who supported the encampments. Some were threatened with sanctions or reprimands, and several student groups were suspended or placed under investigation.

The repression at UQAM was less direct but equally significant. The administration sought to obtain an injunction that would restrict encampment activities and limit its impact on campus. Some actions were violently repressed, particularly during rallies or occupation of strategic spaces on campus. Police presence intensified and students were caught in physical confrontations. Right-wing media outlets, such as QUB radio and Rebel News, in alliance with Zionist institutions like the Centre for Israel and Jewish Affairs (CIJA), waged smear campaigns aimed at discrediting certain activists, accusing them of antisemitism. These media attacks were accompanied by diversionary attempts that included doxxing, jeopardizing the safety of some of those involved.

Faced with these attacks—physical, legal, media-based or administrative—students held fast. In fact, such attempts at intimidation often had the opposite effect, revealing internal institutional contradictions and bolstering solidarity. While Montreal's encampments were among the first in Canada, similar actions had already begun or soon emerged worldwide. By May 2024, the movement had spread to more than 21 Canadian encampments and 150 universities worldwide, making it one of the largest student mobilizations since the 1960s.

Despite the repression, it must be emphasized that the emergence of each encampment constituted a victory in itself. Each encampment generated political force that went far beyond the immediate results.

Unlike many of the encampments around the world, including at McGill, it is also important to highlight the significant political victory achieved at UQAM. On May 29, under growing pressure from the student mobilization and the demands made by activists, the UQAM Board of Directors passed a resolution adopting several of the demands made by the movement.

This victory was only possible because of the tireless work of building strategic alliances with various stakeholders, and ensuring that they were present at the negotiating table alongside the students. The unions, such as the Syndicat des professeurs de l'UQAM (SPUQ) and the Syndicat des professeures et professeurs enseignants de l'UQAM (SPPEUQAM), played a key role by adopting motions in support of the BDS movement during the encampment. This support legitimized encampment demands and pressured the administration, which in turn helped rally more campus members to the cause. Moreover, the participation of student representatives on the UQAM Board of Directors proved to be decisive, as they exerted internal pressure and facilitated compromises and significant progress during negotiations.

Civil society organizations such as Palestinians and Jews United (PAJU) and Independent Jewish Voices (IJV) were crucial to broadening support for the mobilization by reaching out to off-campus groups. The Festival TransAmériques (FTA), which ran concurrently with the encampment, also contributed significantly. This international event added pressure on the university by providing a platform for the encampment representatives at its opening ceremonies, boosting the movement's visibility.

Although the resolution was non-binding, therefore symbolic, it nonetheless was a historic victory that marked a turning point in the response of academic institutions to large-scale mobilization. It underscored the importance of unity, collective commitment, and the need to build strong alliances so that silenced voices will be heard and changes will be made on campus.

Encampments revealed what solidarity with Palestine can cost, but also how politically powerful it is, exposing the vulnerability of institutions torn between their public image and their economic interests. They crystallized a breakthrough in approaches to political organization, revealing a new generation's capacity to reclaim the university as a place of political expression, challenging the existing framework, while rethinking alliances and solidarities. They reminded us that we are here, at the heart of the empire, and that our resistance is part of the same struggle.

These new forms of mobilization, driven by the encampments, are part of a broader dynamic of reorganization of the Palestine solidarity movement, which began well before 2024. A new generation of activists, primarily composed of young people from the Palestinian, Arab, and Muslim communities, has redefined pro-Palestinian engagement, breaking with established codes and imposing decolonial political priorities.

New Generation of Activists: Reorganizing the Struggle, Reinventing Solidarity

The year 2021 marked a turning point in the landscape of Palestine solidarity movements in Montreal, with the emergence of the Palestinian Youth Movement (PYM). Founded in coordination with other North American chapters, this group was distinguished by its exclusively Palestinian and Arab activist composition, a founding principle that set it apart from previous structures. It operated primarily in English, which reflects its roots in transnational networks, and consolidates a shared diasporic perspective across the continent.

Unlike traditional structures, the PYM became a central player in street mobilization, combining political clarity and organizational capacity. By affirming the right of Palestinians to resist, it broke with the more moderate positions of the old structures. Moreover, its approach to mobilization broadened the movement's base by further including Arab and Muslim communities, particularly through mosques, allowing it to reach beyond traditional activist circles.

Almost simultaneously, Montreal for Palestine (M4P) was formed, sharing common bases for mobilization. Although tensions led to a separation, the two groups remained close in their core composition. Their organizational differences appear secondary to the structural evolution they embody within the movement.

October 7, 2023 marked a global tipping point in the struggle for the liberation of Palestine, disrupting the collective political imagination and consolidating new mobilization structures, both elsewhere and in Montreal. The PYM and M4P groups gained legitimacy in this context, becoming key players in weekly mobilizations. They redefined the balance of power and pushed historical actors to adapt to this new dynamic.

While these collectives embodied a new phase in the political organization of solidarity, other historical groups continue to play a key role. PAJU, active since the second Intifada, continues to hold weekly actions in front of the Israeli consulate, a tradition that has even contributed to its relocation from the city centre. Born out of an activist friendship between Rezeq Faraj and Bruce Katz, PAJU remains associated with a generation of progressive leftists, less accessible to new generations.

Independent Jewish Voices (IJV), founded in 2007, is today the leading anti-Zionist Jewish organization in Canada. Rooted in Jewish tradition and committed to combating antisemitism, it is known for its criticism of Zionism and its early support for the BDS campaign. Finally, the student group Solidarité pour les droits humains de Palestinien-nes (SDHPP), active in several Montreal universities, mobilizes young students against their institutions' partnerships with the Zionist entity.

Although the full range of actors involved is difficult to pin down, it is clear that these groups greatly influenced the dynamics after October 7. But to fully understand these reorganizations, it is necessary to situate them within the long history of solidarity with Palestine in Quebec, and within the Quebec political imagination of the past.

Revolutionizing Solidarity for True Collective Liberation

The Quebec sovereignty movement has long been linked to international independence struggles, which, in its early years, fostered an anti-imperialist consciousness, creating fertile ground for political alliances and a commitment to Palestinian liberation.

In 1981, the ruling Parti Québécois, under René Lévesque, became the first political party in North America to welcome representatives of the Palestine Liberation Organization (PLO), which was labeled "terrorist" by Western powers, including Canada. The Parti Québécois affirmed its support for the Palestinian people's right to self-determination.

Although Quebec has often identified with the struggles of the peoples of the Global South, distinguishing itself from the rest of Canada, these moments have been the result of exceptional circumstances. Despite Quebec's historical turning points, it is also a colonial nation with a history that shaped its development, particularly the systematic dispossession and subjugation of Indigenous and enslaved peoples. While Quebec, having not yet consolidated its power, was able to identify with the struggles of colonized peoples, once its power was consolidated, it rediscovered its colonial position, aligning itself with imperialist forces.

Recently, a much narrower nationalist movement has emerged in Quebec, shifting from a broad social project towards one that is merely focused on carving out a capitalist "nation" distinct only in language. This is evidenced by the current Quebec government's unconditional support for wars and genocide, among other things, particularly in Gaza.

It is important to re-situate ourselves in the struggles of the peoples of the Global South, for it is these struggles that still carry the true hopes for transformation. As Frantz Fanon so aptly put it: "Each generation must, in relative opacity, confront its mission: fulfill it or betray it." Today, in the heart of the Empire, we have the opportunity to seize this mission and realize it, and our compass must always point to the South, where true revolutions are played out.

In a world that is reeling, choosing a side is no longer a luxury: it is a collective responsibility. We have chosen for future generations, for those who can no longer speak, and to avoid betraying our memories. We have acted, resisted, and confronted. If we have held on, it is also so that history will remember that in the face of horror, we did not give in.

This fight is not only for Palestine, but for the dignity of all oppressed peoples. Every act of resistance is a building block for collective liberation. What we have begun, others will continue—those who believe that injustice must never be accepted, that the freedom of peoples is an arduous but indispensable task. Together, in memory and in action, we march until justice is achieved.

CHAPTER 13

When Human Rights are "Made by McGill"*

Ehab Lotayef

In 2024, the January 29th Quebec City mosque massacre commemoration event at McGill University became a forum for students to speak up against the university administration's position regarding the genocide that had been going on in Gaza for months. As the moderator of the online event, I gave the student speakers as much room as I could to voice their criticism and concerns which were, in my opinion, both timely and valid.

In January 2025, I was to pay the price.

Let me start from the beginning. From the first message that the new president of McGill, Deep Saini, sent to the McGill community (on October 12, 2023), it was obvious that the administration did not intend to take a balanced or fair position regarding the Israeli/Palestinian conflict

* "Made by McGill" is a marketing slogan adopted by the university in 2019.

or the two communities affected by what was happening in the Middle East: "I have watched with horror the immense suffering and loss of human life that Hamas caused through its heinous terrorist attack on Israel. This act, and the continuing violence in Israel and Gaza, have created profound distress within McGill." There was no reference to Israel's indiscriminate bombing of civilians and the collective punishment of Gazans which had already begun.

In a subsequent message on November 1, the president addressed the suffering of both peoples without referring to the disproportionate human loss on one side nor pointing to Israel as the perpetrator of anything—as if the death of over 7,000 civilians was caused by a natural disaster, not by Israel's indiscriminate bombing.

During the days between the release of those two communiques, I exchanged emails and met with members of the McGill leadership team to discuss the imbalance of the university position towards its various Jewish, Palestinian, and Arab communities. After one meeting, where there was no acknowledgement of any imbalance, I adapted the president's words to formulate a sympathy message for the Palestinian and Arab members of the McGill community, and offered that this be disseminated on behalf of the university. While my suggestion was acknowledged, neither my letter nor its sentiment were ever reflected in any message sent by the university.

And although we (a group of McGill academics and staff) continued to meet and exchange with members of the university leadership team over the subsequent months, voicing the same and other concerns, we were listened to but never heard.

As the Israeli genocide of the civilian population of Gaza continued unabated, temperatures rose on campus as they did across Montreal, throughout the country, and around the world. The position of the McGill administration, however, did not shift.

In February 2024, a group of McGill University students initiated a hunger strike to protest the university's investments in companies linked to the Israeli military. The hunger strikers and their supporters demanded that McGill divest from various companies, including defense contractors like Lockheed Martin and Safran, which supply equipment to Israel. Despite saying the right thing and expressing concern about the health of the students, the administration did nothing to actively address their concerns or demands.

In April 2024, matters heated up with the establishment of a pro-Palestinian encampment on McGill's lower field. Overnight, the McGill administration became openly antagonistic towards Palestinian students, staff, and their supporters. From that point on, no further meaningful communication took place with the McGill administration regarding Gaza or Palestine.

While other universities (e.g., UQAM, McMaster, and University of Ottawa) took a more friendly and open position towards pro-Palestinian encampments on their grounds, negotiating settlements that satisfied the students, McGill took a confrontational position that threatened students and threw at them unproven accusations.

On July 10, 2024, the McGill community woke up to a message from the administration saying that the downtown campus was closed. Despite failing to obtain a court injunction to dismantle the encampment, and after the city and Montreal police refused to get involved, the McGill administration hired Groupe Sirco, a private security firm (dare I say paramilitary) to clear the encampment. The clearing took days and the campus, or parts of it, were closed for weeks. The area felt like a war zone.

While the campus grounds eventually got back to normal, the environment and sentiments within the McGill community remain bruised and will take years to heal.

Let me get back to where I started. In the months following the Quebec City mosque massacre in 2017, I was among members of the McGill community who advocated for the planting of a tree and placing a plaque on the McGill grounds to commemorate the victims of the shootings by a deranged and racist young man. I was also among those who suggested holding an annual commemoration of the massacre at McGill on January 29th of each year. I emceed each and every one of those commemorations, whether held in person or virtually, until 2024.

But come 2025, the university administration wanted to have a stronger grip on what happens and what is said in that event. They changed it from a forum for students and staff to a lecture given by an outside guest who had no connection to what had been happening on campus. I was given the symbolic role of leading a procession to lay flowers at the commemorative plaque, but no opportunity to speak about the actions of the McGill administration or voice any concern or opinion I might have about the University. I replied to their invitation with the following message:

> Thank you for inviting me to have a role in this important commemoration, which I am proud to have helped initiate

> many years ago, and was always involved in planning for, organizing, and presenting.
>
> Yet, unfortunately, due to my profound disagreement with how the McGill administration handled what has been happening in Gaza and how it dealt with, and stifles, members of the McGill community who speak out for Palestinian rights, I respectfully decline to have any official role in this year's commemoration as I believe that supporting human rights and exposing injustices should not be selective.

As was the case regarding many struggles for justice that I witnessed during my lifetime—African American Rights, Native Rights, Vietnam, etc.—most institutions only support a just cause when it becomes mainstream. Only a few brave and conscience-led institutions take the risk and move without delay to support causes that are not yet popular among their donors and backers. Those are the ones that change the world for the better. Unfortunately, McGill is far from being on the vanguard of human rights and just causes.

Photo: Sean Tucker

CHAPTER 14

Silence about Gaza in UBC's School of Population and Public Health

Sean Tucker

> The best way to defend academic freedom is to use it.
>
> —Shannon Dea, Dean of Arts, University of Regina

I am a part-time university professor at the University of Regina and, until 2024, I was also a sessional lecturer at the University of British Columbia. Growing up in an evangelical Christian home, I don't recall Israel or Palestine ever being discussed in my family, at church, or in public school. Despite this, my default yet uninformed world view was pro-Israel.

More generally, oppression was not often talked about in my family. My grandparents lived in apartheid Rhodesia (now Zimbabwe) during the brutal war for independence that ended in 1979. Somewhere there is a photo of me as a three-year-old wearing a T-shirt that says "Rhodesia is super" and "I'm behind Rhodesia." I also had extended family living in apartheid South Africa. As a 16-year-old visitor to the country in 1990, I do not recall discussions about either racism or white supremacy. Only now are some family members beginning to have these conversations.

The first time I remember being confronted with Israel's military occupation was in October 2001. At the time, I was dating someone who actively supported Palestinian human rights and self-determination. I remember my reaction to a small button on my girlfriend's backpack: "I support the Intifada." Even though I knew very little about current events and the decades of suffering experienced by Palestinians, I scoffed at the pin, falsely equating the word Intifada (meaning uprising or shaking off) with terrorism.

My ignorance persisted until 2014. That was when my faculty at the University of Regina pursued a partnership with the Policing and Homeland Security Studies Program at Hebrew University in Israel. The plan was for students in a new MBA in Public Safety program to enroll in courses in counterterrorism and intelligence gathering, and participate in a "public safety" study tour in Israel.[1] The partnership was as much a political project as it was academic—it was supported by the then-Saskatchewan premier Brad Wall, the Centre for Israel and Jewish Affairs (CIJA), and Israel's ambassador to Canada.[2] Colleagues who were knowledgeable about the tactics of the pro-Israel lobby in Canada sounded the alarm.

I became quite upset that my school was blindly entering into an agreement to create a program that would legitimize Israel's occupation and system of apartheid among our graduate students. To make matters worse, the negotiations with Hebrew University coincided with the 2014 assault on Gaza, which resulted in the deaths of over 1,100 Palestinian and 6 Israeli civilians.

A broad coalition of students, faculty, and community organizations mobilized under the banner "Coalition to Free Palestine" to pressure the University of Regina to end the partnership. In protest, I resigned from teaching graduate courses.

It was through this campaign that friends, colleagues and Arab students helped me begin to understand Israel's decades-long military occupation. Part of my unlearning included reading testimonies of former IDF soldiers who witnessed or participated in human rights abuses of Palestinians.[3] This incident at the University of Regina marked a major turning point in my understanding of oppression and the history of Palestine and Israel.

Eventually, the partnership with Hebrew University folded, quietly.[4] To my knowledge, there were no repercussions for those who publicly spoke out against the agreement.

A decade later, in 2024, I had a very different experience as a sessional lecturer at the School of Population and Public Health (SPPH) in the UBC Faculty of Medicine. Throughout Israel's genocide in Gaza, the school and most faculty members avoided the issue. An open letter from a group of public health students put it this way:

> ...We witnessed and experienced first-hand the culture of silence at SPPH and the chilling effect that has been pervasive across UBC-Vancouver, on the topic of Israel's genocidal war on Gaza and the occupied West Bank. Not only did SPPH remain silent, but the School did not provide any resources to students who may have been directly impacted by these events happening overseas. The complete silence and lack of care at SPPH have been clear.[5]

In response to requests from some students in my leadership class to learn about the public health emergency in Gaza, and to raise awareness about silence in the school, I wrote letters to UBC leaders, co-organized events, and was involved in disseminating information, including postering in the school. These forms of voice were unwelcome by the school and eventually the decision was made to not reappoint me. Even though I knew advocacy for education around Palestine came with risks, I was surprised that I was essentially fired for exercising my academic freedom. I detailed my experience in this open letter to the president, provost, dean of medicine, and SPPH director at the University of British Columbia:

> January 2, 2025
>
> Dear Drs. Bacon, Averill, Kelleher, and Anis,
>
> I am writing in regards to the UBC School of Population and Public Health's (SPPH) decision to dismiss me from my teaching position, and to respectfully ask that you act upon calls from students, alumni, faculty, and other individuals and organizations, to reinstate me to teach this term. Although I filed a complaint through the UBC Faculty Association, this matter is not simply a labour relations issue. Reversing the decision about my termination would send a positive message to the UBC community that UBC does indeed stand by its commitment to academic freedom and promoting learning on issues of global importance.
>
> In 2022, I was invited to redesign and, going forward, teach an SPPH course in leadership. I was asked to facilitate student learning and self-reflection about public health leadership values and practice. However, I learned that exercising these values in relation to the ongoing atrocities in Gaza was unwelcome in the school—so much so that it cost me my job.
>
> Over the course of the past year, it became apparent to me and others that there was a need within SPPH to discuss

the public health situation in Gaza in the context of the school's commitment to health equity. Attempts to facilitate this, and SPPH's responses, are summarized below:

- When, in January 2024, several students in my leadership class expressed concern that discussion about the humanitarian emergency in Gaza was off limits in the school, I shared these concerns, and my own observations about the silence surrounding the topic, in a letter to the SPPH leadership team (attached below). I received no reply.
- Weeks later, I supported an SPPH student screening of the critically-acclaimed film *Israelism* (2023)—a film made by Jewish American youth about changing values and growing concerns within the Jewish community regarding the treatment of Palestinians. We were informed that the UBC Risk Management team had flagged the event as a risk and that the date of the screening may need to be delayed to accommodate a review. Fortunately, we were able to negotiate a room booking for the event, but we were required to have two campus security personnel present. (I note that there have been several showings of this film at universities in BC; to my knowledge, there have never been any security incidents.)
- In February, a group of SPPH students organized an event entitled "Global Health and the War on Gaza: Starting the Conversation in the SPPH Community." The organizers were denied access to the school's newsletter and email listserv to promote this important event to the broader SPPH community.
- In April 2024, SPPH declined to sponsor an event featuring a speaker from Save the Children ("The impact of war on children in Gaza," co-sponsored by other schools and departments at UBC). At that time, my co-organizer and I learned there was also an unwritten policy that

prohibits events focused on Gaza from being advertised in SPPH's newsletter. We asked why SPPH chose not to sponsor our event when every other UBC school/department that was invited to sponsor the event did so. I was told that the University Act did not allow the school's leadership or the school itself to sponsor events related to the Israel and Gaza conflict. It is noteworthy that other schools and departments did not share this interpretation of the Act.

- In May 2024, following several requests to meet with the school's director, I was told that he was open to an in person meeting. Campus is an 8-hour round trip for me and so I requested a remote meeting via Zoom. I was told that there were concerns about the security of Zoom for discussion of this sensitive topic. To facilitate a virtual meeting, I offered to sign a confidentiality agreement. My offer wasn't responded to. I regret that we were unable to find a suitable time to meet on campus and a virtual meeting wasn't an option.
- To counter the silence in the school and raise awareness about malnutrition, disease, and the slaughter of Palestinian children in Gaza, colleagues and I posted direct official quotes from Save the Children, UNICEF, and Doctors without Borders on SPPH bulletin boards.[6] In an apparent response to these posters, the SPPH management team later adopted a new bulletin policy that states, in part, that posters will be removed if they "may contribute" to an "uncomfortable environment."
- In late-August 2024, I wrote an op-ed in *The Tyee* about the need for universities to play a more active role in facilitating learning and discussion about Palestine and Israel.[7] It was well-received in the public sphere and consistent with what other academic scholars have been saying in popular newspapers and academic journals.

In early-September 2024, I was invited with other Occupational and Environmental Hygiene (OEH) teaching faculty to attend a student orientation luncheon, where I introduced myself as the leadership course instructor. Five weeks later, I was informed via a phone call that I would no longer be teaching the leadership course. I asked for reconsideration and, in a follow-up email, I was told that the leadership course was no longer needed. (I note that a stakeholder consultation had found that leadership was one of the most frequently identified gaps in the OEH program.) However, I later learned that the course was not in fact cancelled, and is being offered on Wednesdays during the upcoming Winter term.

Importantly, there have been no concerns within OEH about my teaching performance. I am convinced, as are the many organizations and individuals that have reached out to you, that the decision to terminate my appointment is a consequence of my efforts to raise awareness about the public health disaster in Gaza.

Amnesty International, Human Rights Watch, Doctors without Borders, Oxfam, Save the Children, UNICEF, and other internationally-respected NGOs have issued reports documenting wide-ranging human rights atrocities committed by Israel in Gaza: restriction of access to water, food, and medical supplies; indiscriminate bombing of civilian populations; targeting of children; and targeting health care workers and infrastructure (hospitals). In November 2024, arrest warrants were issued by the International Criminal Court for the Prime Minister of Israel and one of his senior ministers for probable war crimes.

I, along with many members of the UBC community feel that it is unconscionable that a school of public health that aspires to be a leader in global public health would actively avoid discussions about any humanitarian crisis on the scale of what is unfolding in Gaza.

> SPPH's decision to dismiss an outspoken sessional lecturer only amplifies uncomfortable questions about the school's silence about the ongoing genocide in Gaza: Who does our silence serve? Why is there a Palestine exception? What example are we setting for our future medical and public health leaders?
>
> The school must foster a culture where it is safe for students and faculty to express public health values without fear of reprisal. It is, therefore, important that the school and UBC reaffirm their commitment to academic freedom, freedom of expression, and tolerance of dissent. Universities cannot credibly fulfill their mission otherwise. The response from the larger community of UBC alumni, faculty, students and community groups in my support emphasizes these points.
>
> Again, I urge you to abide by the stated mission of SPPH and the University by promoting honest, respectful discussion about the devastation of public health in Gaza, and to reinstate me to my teaching position this term.[8]
>
> Thank you,
> Sean Tucker, PhD

People often ask me where the pressure to refrain from speaking about the atrocities in Gaza comes from at UBC. I honestly don't know.[9] What I can say is that based on my own observations and speaking with students, staff, and faculty is that the Palestine exception is real and pervasive at UBC, especially in the medical school. At UBC, I know first-hand of instances where Palestinian students faced barriers booking meeting rooms; of a weak commitment to investigating certain incidents of anti-Palestinian and anti-Muslim discrimination; and unprecedented security and surveillance of peaceful protest and expression. In February 2025, RCMP officers went to the office of the UBC student paper, the *Ubyssey*, "seeking contact information for sources in a previous story, who they anticipated might stage a [pro-Palestine] demonstration."[10] There are other incidents that I cannot comment on for privacy reasons.

I am grateful for the support of these individuals and groups: Emily Eaton, Fernwood Publishing, Avi Lewis, Jerry Spiegel, Andrew Stevens, UBC Faculty for Palestine, UBC Independent Jewish Voices, UBC Jewish Faculty Network, University of Toronto Public Health for Palestine, Annalee Yassi, Val Zink, and several other courageous students, and colleagues whom I cannot name for safety reasons.

What can be done to counteract fear and silencing on campuses? As we are able, we should align our actions with our values. Solidarity is our strength and so finding allies and sticking together during the tough times of pro-Palestinian activism is critically important. If we find ourselves in a position of privilege, we must use our privilege to stand with and support others. While there have been consequences for me, the consequences for others (Palestinian-Canadian, Muslim, precariously employed) far outweigh anything I have (or ever will) experience.

University and college faculty members with tenure have an important role in protecting students and their untenured and precariously employed colleagues from malicious attacks and smear campaigns. We can also use collegial governance processes to challenge the Palestine exception wherever it exists in the academy.

We must avoid the trap of self-censorship. If we receive pushback for exercising academic freedom, we should seek representation from our union and/or the Canadian

Association of University Teachers and draw on support from local solidarity campaigns.

Universities must continue to be places for exploring difficult issues. Ontario Justice Markus Koehnen acknowledged this in his decision regarding the legality of the spring 2024 pro-Palestinian encampment at the University of Toronto:

> To the extent that these [reputational] harms arise because the protest has focused attention on a divisive issue, that is something all residents of a free and democratic society must be prepared to live with. That is all the more the case in a university whose mandate it [is] to explore difficult issues.[11]

There is still work to do to overcome resistance to exploring critical questions about an issue that some say is "too complex" and "too divisive." We cannot allow ourselves to be distracted—we must rise to the challenge, continue to ask inconvenient questions, and exercise our academic freedom and freedom of expression.

Notes

1. "A blatant disregard of ethics," the *Carillon*, 30 January 2024.
2. "U of R continues to seek controversial partnership," the *Carillon*, 26 February 2014.
3. *Our Harsh Logic: Israeli Soldiers' Testimonies from the Occupied Territories 2000-2010*. Breaking the Silence, Metropolitan Books, New York, 2012.
4. "University of Regina rejects Hebrew University collaboration," *CBC News*, 13 August 2014.
5. Statement on Silence at SPPH: Student Experience, Instagram, 29 January 2025.
6. A number of people later told me that there were allegations that the posters were perceived by some as "hate speech" because they included the statement "Who does our silence serve?"

7. Sean Tucker, "When discussing Israel and Palestine, Universities must do better," *The Tyee*, 23 August 2024.
8. In February 2025, the UBC Faculty Association submitted a 10-page written grievance to the UBC Provost. UBC formally replied in May 2025. At the time of publication, there is no resolution to the grievance. The matter may be referred to a formal arbitration hearing in which case there will be a written decision that I hope will be made public.
9. The UBC chapter of Jewish Faculty Network offered this view: "We were shocked to learn that Professor Tucker was recently abruptly removed from this teaching assignment and are deeply concerned that the decision for the removal relates largely to his advocacy for more learning and discussion about Palestine and Israel. We are aware that the university is being lobbied intensely to silence discussion of what is happening in Gaza, and we strongly suspect that the decision regarding Professor Tucker is linked to his activities in this regard."
10. Spencer Izen, "'I have questions': UBC staffer speaks out after RCMP detained him while walking past Invictus Games wearing a keffiyeh," *Ubyssey*, 5 March 2025.
11. Citation, Ontario Superior Court of Justice. Between The Governing Council of the University of Toronto and (varia) Respondents, 2 July 2024.

CHAPTER 15

No to Weaponizing Antisemitism

Open Letter in *La Presse* from Jewish Faculty in Quebec

The following open letter was written and signed by Jewish faculty across Quebec in the spring of 2025 in response to political interference in the CEGEP (junior college) system.

In August 2024, before the start of the fall semester, Higher Education Minister Pascale Déry had attempted to interfere in the content of upcoming courses at Dawson and Vanier Colleges because they included material related to Palestine. Toward the end of that same semester, Déry had invoked her power under the Loi sur les collèges d'enseignement général et professionnel to launch an unprecedented public inquiry into these same two colleges. Prior to this letter's publication, media scrutiny of Dery's actions had focused primarily on the danger they posed to academic freedom. Our letter echoed these concerns while also pointing to the government's weaponization of antisemitism, used to silence Palestinian voices.

The letter, published on April 11, 2025 in *La Presse,* received significant attention. It was covered by *La Presse, Radio Canada, Le Devoir, CTV News,* the *Rover,* and other media in Quebec. Over the course of spring 2025, 14 teachers' unions published motions calling for Déry's resignation, many directly citing our letter. And on May 20, 2025, the letter was read out loud to Minister Déry in the National Assembly by MNA Sol Zanetti. In the months following its publication, dozens of unions and organizations joined the call for Déry's resignation, as did over 1,000 CEGEP and university professors in a letter to *Le Devoir.*

The reach and impact of this open letter reveals the importance of speaking out, as Jews with diverse backgrounds and perspectives, against the conflation of antisemitism and anti-Zionism, which is wielded to silence dissent and justify violence in our names. The letter also underscores the importance of organizing together as faculty across CEGEPs and universities to collectively defend our institutions of higher education against censorship, repression, and anti-Palestinian racism.

Shira Avni, Concordia University
Michael Blum, Université du Québec à Montréal
Danielle Bobker, Concordia University
Lara Braitstein, McGill University
Noah Brender, Dawson College
Kevin Gould, Concordia University
Sara Louise Kendall, Dawson College
Natalie Kouri-Towe, Concordia University
Nadia Moss, Dawson College
Yakov Rabkin, Université de Montréal
Itay Sapir, Université du Québec à Montréal
Daniel Schwartz, McGill University
Jeremy Stolow, Concordia University
Mark Sussman, Concordia University
Katherine Zien, McGill University
Anya Zilberstein, Concordia University

We write as Jewish professors based at Quebec universities and CEGEPS.[1]

In December 2024, Minister of Higher Education Pascale Déry announced an investigation into the political climate at Dawson and Vanier Colleges, taking administrations at both CEGEPs by surprise. The only grounds Déry gave for this unprecedented inquiry were confidential student complaints, which no one outside the Ministry has seen because they did not go through ordinary channels. The Centre for Israel and Jewish Affairs (CIJA), a pro-Israel lobby group on whose board Déry served from 2016 to 2022, has publicly taken credit for mobilizing these complaints and lobbying Déry to act on them.

Journalists also discovered recently that Déry had summoned the Directors General of Dawson and Vanier to defend the content of two particular literature courses because they featured Palestinian authors—a shocking deviation from normal procedures and a clear violation of the government's own principles on academic freedom. These inappropriate interventions, like the investigation Déry launched in December, seem intended to silence Palestinian voices, to stifle discussion of Palestine in and out of the classroom, and to intimidate teachers and students who support Palestinian human rights—many of whom are Jewish.

As Jewish faculty, we know that Jewish students are not endangered by reading Palestinian authors. Nor is their safety threatened by expressions of solidarity with Palestine, particularly at a time when leading human rights organizations such as Amnesty International and Human Rights Watch describe Israel's actions in Gaza as genocide. Support for Palestinian human rights is not antisemitic, and we are profoundly disturbed to see the concept of antisemitism being distorted to attack academic freedom and suppress political protest. We view this as a direct threat to our ability to fight actual antisemitism in this province.

Minister Déry's actions show that she is unfit to serve as Minister of Higher Education. We therefore call for her immediate resignation. Further, we call on the Quebec government to immediately end the investigations into Vanier and Dawson and commit to respecting teachers' academic freedom and students' freedom of expression at colleges and universities across the province. Finally, as Jewish scholars we demand that the Ministry stop weaponizing antisemitism to justify attacks on Palestinians and their allies in Quebec.

Note

1. Quebec's CEGEP (college d'enseignement général et professionnel) system was founded in 1967 to provide free and accessible post-secondary education. Programs are typically two or three years depending on whether they are academic, leading to university, or technical, leading to a certification.

CHAPTER 16

Beyond the Pale, Beyond the Fringe: Voices from the Jewish Faculty Network*

Abigail B. Bakan, Mo Pareles, Jillian Rogin,
Lesley Wood, Anna Zalik

LEILA MARSHY: In 2021, you wrote about the need for academic freedom for scholars, particularly Jewish scholars, on the issue of Israel/Palestine, and that the IHRA definition of antisemitism was an impediment. Can you explain this?

ABBIE B. BAKAN AND MO PARELES: The International Holocaust Remembrance Alliance (IHRA) working definition of antisemitism, adopted in 2016, is remarkably vague: "Antisemitism is a certain perception of Jews, which may be expressed as hatred toward Jews. Rhetorical and physical manifestations of antisemitism are directed toward Jewish or non-Jewish individuals and/or their property, toward Jewish community institutions and religious facilities."

---

* The Jewish Faculty Network is a national network of Jewish Canadian academics: www.jewishfaculty.ca

It is followed by a list of 11 examples, 7 of which refer explicitly or implicitly to the state of Israel. The definition as a whole, including the examples, forwards the false equation of Judaism with the state of Israel, which is not about challenging antisemitism at all. Instead, it premises a Zionist political perspective that assumes Jews and non-Jews cannot live together in a democratic state, and therefore naturalizes the Nakba.

Where the IHRA definition has been adopted in universities, often explicitly in the US and Europe and implicitly in Canada, the effect has been detrimental to scholarship in a number of ways. Its application has threatened academic freedom and advanced racist stereotypes against Palestinians and supporters of Palestinian rights, and suppressed Palestinian narratives and true accounts of Palestinian history in favour of pro-Israel narratives. We have experienced and observed these effects personally on our campuses, including in the 2021 removal of an appointment offer for legal scholar Valentina Azarova at the University of Toronto.

The false equating of antisemitism with criticism of the state of Israel imposes dangerous limits on what can be taught and written about Israel and Palestine. This harms not only academic freedom's role in advancing effective scholarship and teaching but the quality of education for undergraduate and graduate students. Actions in support of Palestine on university campuses, such as the student encampments calling for universities to divest from Israeli companies involved in war crimes, are similarly falsely charged with antisemitism. This climate of repression also leads to silencing and targeting of Palestinian scholars and students and others (including Jews and Israelis) who research Palestine. Such scholarly research cannot freely be shared and those who advance it face challenges in grants and future scholarship.

Moreover, actual antisemitism is not challenged by this definition. Jewish scholars, and scholars in Jewish studies, find themselves in situations where Jewishness itself is absurdly under surveillance. Even raising the spectre that Israel, Zionism, or a related topic might be discussed produces scrutiny, surveillance and censorship.

One paradigmatic case among many is that of Professor Matthew Berkman of Oberlin College, who was targeted by a right-wing group called Mothers Against Antisemitism. Berkman, a Jewish person who had been involved with the activist group Jewish Voice for Peace, taught a Jewish studies course called "Jews and Power." In this and similar cases, the scrutiny that anti-education and right-wing groups apply to the study of gender, sexuality, racialization, climate, and Palestine has also impacted the study of Jewishness, Jewish political life, and Jewish studies.

As Jewish academics who participate in Jewish life and are educated in Jewish histories of left-wing struggle and solidarity, we know that "antisemite," as well as "self-hating" and ruder terms originating in the Nazi era, are now applied to leftist Jews without reference to their literal meaning but rather to mean "politically undesirable." This explains why United States Representative Elise Stefanik (R-NY), a right-wing Christian nationalist, retains on her website a statement accusing Jewish Harvard professor Derek Penslar, a senior Jewish studies scholar, of "despicable antisemitic views and statements." It is not that Jewish scholars are more in need of academic freedom than anyone else; it is only that the use of the term "antisemitism" to curb Jewish progressive speech by people who passionately hate Jewish people is so hideously and profoundly ironic.

The ludicrous logic of IHRA has not yet altogether prevailed. The Canadian Association of University Teachers (CAUT), which represents university faculty associations and unions across Canada, has rejected IHRA as a "significant threat to academic freedom at Canadian universities and colleges." Universities in Australia appear reluctant to endorse IHRA, also citing academic freedom and perhaps recognizing the futility of appeasing anti-academic forces. IHRA will be defeated—sooner or later.

The trope of the "Jewish lobby" has long been a bellwether for identifying antisemitism and conspiracy theories, and emboldening discrimination. Yet the Israeli lobby is not only real and impactful, it is distinct from the so-called Jewish lobby. Can you help us parse this? Why is it critical that this distinction is made not only for ourselves, but for the media and institutions around us?

JILLIAN ROGIN: Antisemitic tropes about Jewish power, conspiracy theories about Jewish control, and beliefs that Jews are orchestrating world domination, were popularized with the publication of the Protocols of the Elders of Zion at the turn of the 20th century and continue to abound.

These forms of antisemitism are often drawn upon to describe the pro-Israel lobby in Canada and elsewhere in the struggle to name and identify entities, groups, and individuals that support and uphold Israeli violence against Palestinians. Characterizing the pro-Israel lobby as Jewish, powerful, and controlling and driving government policy, and depicting Jews as having a dual loyalty with respect to Israel, repeats antisemitism. It also obscures important historic and ongoing dynamics that contribute to the atmosphere of repression currently taking hold in Canada and elsewhere that combine to create support for the state of Israel. Analytic clarity is needed to parse the myriad individuals, groups, and organizations that operate to support and uphold Israeli state interests and to understand the ways in which the state of Israel launders its human rights abuses through lobbying efforts.

The pro-Israel lobby is dominated by Christian Zionism, adherents of which number approximately 600,000,000 worldwide. In the United States, upwards of 80 million people identify as Christian Zionists, and evangelical Christian Zionism is hugely influential in American politics. The military industrial complex in North America and elsewhere strongly aligns with the Israeli military industrial complex through arms deals, security apparatus exchange, and military technology sharing. For example, a recent report details a $78.8 million dollar contract awarded to a Canadian Crown corporation to provide the United States Department of Defence with artillery propellants that will be supplied to Israel—this in the midst of an ongoing genocide against Palestinians and contradicting Canada's commitment to halting arms sales to Israel.[1] The history of the formation of the state of Israel is a history of British imperial and colonial interests combining to create widespread support and these interests continue to animate current ideological and material US and western support for Israeli violence.

At the same time, Jewish-identified pro-Israel lobby groups advocate for changes to law and policy in ways that weaponize antisemitism, erode civil liberties, and operate to silence Palestinians and their supporters (including Jewish allies). Questions about the power and influence of Jewish pro-Israel lobby groups—*How are they so successful in their efforts? How do they wield so much power?*—are simply misguided for they both elide important dynamics that contribute to the atmosphere of repression currently taking hold in Canada and also risk emphasizing "Jewish power" and conspiracy tropes.

The more prescient questions are: Why do politicians, academic institutions, law enforcement agencies, and policy and law makers listen to the pro-Israel lobby, including Jewish-identified lobby groups? What investments do these entities have in upholding support for the Israeli state and the unspeakable racist-motivated violence it has unleashed against Palestinians currently and historically? Why do some institutions and individuals in Canada so gravely fear the "wrath" of the Jewish pro-Israel lobby when in fact, Jewish people in Canada make up a tiny portion of the population? Is this an actual instance where antisemitism manifests in fear of the perceived power of Jewish people that inspires acquiescence?

There are certainly powerful lobby groups in Canada that have vast resources that are not able to achieve the kind of gains that pro-Israel lobbyists enjoy. Unions, for example, are larger in number and likely have more resources than all of the pro-Israel groups in Canada combined. And yet, we don't see unions enjoying the same scale of successes in terms of lobbying efforts.

Turning our attention back on those who are receptive, listening attentively to what pro-Israel groups have to say, is crucially important. Did former Prime Minister Justin Trudeau openly identify as a Zionist due to pressure from pro-Israel lobby groups? Or did he do so to proclaim Canada's investments and shared interests in Israeli state structures of violence? Or maybe he did so out of fear of an inflated perception of "Jewish power."

Paying attention to the varied responses to pro-Israel Jewish lobbying elucidates far more critical and nuanced results than questioning the power of the lobby itself. We ought to turn our attention to those that pick up what the pro-Israel lobby groups put down.

The importance and impact of Jewish individuals and groups in combatting this war cannot be underestimated. From Israeli scholars and activists, to average people here in Canada and elsewhere, Jews have been a critical element to lending voice and legitimacy to the Palestinian movement. But has there been a cost to this? I look at Palestinian activists and I see communities forging together. I look at my Jewish friends and I see families breaking apart. Can you talk about the risks, costs and, hopefully one day, rewards of being Jewish and advocating for Palestinian liberation?

LESLEY WOOD: There were Jewish activists committed to Palestinian liberation before October 7, 2023, but since October 7 there are far more, and we are much more visible. The Jewish community is transforming. Despite relative consistency in Jewish identity and practice across generations in Canada, this past year and a half has exacerbated divisions, shifted political affinities and created new organizations and institutions. Surveys show that while Canadian Jewish voters are shifting to the right, the emotional connection many Jews feel with Israel is declining.[2]

Despite this, being a visible pro-Palestinian Jew puts one outside the mainstream of Jewish life and institutions. One risks losing family and friends. It means strained relationships. It generates challenges to one's identity as a "real Jew." It may even lead others to accuse one of antisemitism or self-hatred. To be exiled from one's own community. Beyond the grief that this generates, it creates a political dilemma. Does one continue to mobilize as a Jew, to spend energy challenging the Zionist claim to represent all Jews, fighting for influence in the Jewish community and risking making internecine community battles too central during a genocide? Or does one continue to support Palestinian liberation through work challenging Israel and the complicity of other actors from outside of the Jewish community?

Many Palestinian activists have asked Jews acting in solidarity to continue to identify visibly and volubly as Jews; to embrace our Jewish identity while fighting for Palestine. While Jewishness is not about how observant one is, this choice has led some of us, especially those of us who are secular leftists, into more active Jewish practice. For example, the shabbat prayers held during the Palestinian solidarity encampments became a weekly anchor and a space to learn ritual. Our effort to challenge the Zionist representation of the Jewish community over decades has nurtured newer formations like the Jewish Faculty Network in 2021, and, since October 2023, Jews Say No to Genocide, among others. These new groups have allowed for more focused discussions about Israel's path and our responsibility. The period since 2023 also saw new energy and new members joining pre-existing groups like the United Jewish People's Order, Independent Jewish Voices, and If Not Now. Some of these groups are actively collaborating with formations in other countries and there is a flourishing cultural re-engagement with submerged anti-Zionist Jewish diasporic traditions.

Although emerging out of grief and a sense of responsibility, one of the most rewarding elements of being active as a Jew for Palestinian liberation has been the deepening relationships that many of us have had with Palestinians. In the past year, we have learned more about Palestinian culture, politics, and practices. Where one door closes, another opens.

Countless academics, including yourself, are accused on the Canary Mission website of "demonizing Israel." What is the Canary Mission? Should we be worried about it?

ANNA ZALIK: The genocidal war on Palestine is occurring alongside a broader crisis of liberal democratic institutions and the late-20th-century global geopolitical order. We have seen the contours of this crisis emerging since the 2008 financial crisis, if not since 2001 and the "Global War on Terror" that followed 9/11. Over the past two years, the doxxing that Palestine advocates endure via sites like Canary Mission set up by Israel lobby organizations has been overshadowed by the extension of police-state power aiming to criminalize peaceful protest for Palestine. As documented in detail elsewhere in this volume, this has entailed significant repression of student protesters—among others—through threats and actual expulsions of both domestic and international students, kangaroo court-like hearings under the rubric of "student codes of conduct," substantial fines directed at students,[3] and violent evictions[4] of encampments,[5] including at York University,[6] where I teach. Across Canada, many examples could be cited, among them the prosecution of the Indigo 11,[7] as well as numerous other arrests and charges against Palestine solidarity protesters.

Some years prior to these events, in 2019, I was added to the list of the Canary Mission, described by the Committee on Academic Freedom of the Middle East Studies Association as a "secretive, but clearly non-academic political organization"[8] aimed at pursuing defamatory attacks against university and college faculty and students who mobilize in support of Palestinian rights. Like the organization HonestReporting, Canary Mission acts as a pro-Israel watchdog and intimidation body.[9] I assume, although this is not itemized on the "profile" posted on their site, that my participation in the York University Advisory Committee on Responsible Investment (YUACRI) led to my name being added to the site. YUACRI was suspended[10] by senior York University administrators in 2017 after the committee voted to endorse two university-community-led petitions, one on arms divestment (led by the YUDIVEST coalition), the other on fossil fuel divestment (led by Fossil Free York). The YUDIVEST petition was perceived as advancing the Boycott, Divestment and Sanctions movement and was therefore subject to particular scrutiny and pushback, although it appeared that the York University Board of Governors was equally concerned about the Fossil Free petition. At the time, the committee's suspension was quite extraordinary given that YUACRI held only an advisory position vis-à-vis the York University Board of Governors and had no substantive control over financial decisions. One could only speculate that the university's Board of Governors did not wish to find themselves in the awkward position of having to recuse themselves from voting for or against our advice due to a conflict of interest. This seemed probable given that various members held senior positions, or may have been otherwise tied to, financial institutions, legal firms and related bodies directly invested in or profiting from the weapons industry and/or fossil fuel industry.

Despite the formal "suspension" of YUACRI, members of the committee, including myself, went on to submit our final report in support of the implementation of the YUDIVEST petition for weapons divestment in 2018.[11] The university community's vocal protest against the administration's attempt to block a consultative process that the senior administration had itself established spoke volumes about purportedly democratic practices and collegial governance at the university.

Since October 2023, numerous academics have been added to various lists and sublists prepared by Canary Mission. This includes faculty members who have spoken at student encampments for Palestine, or who simply supported students' right to free speech. In the context of the Trump administration's targeting of pro-Palestine speech as the bludgeon for attacking institutions and research bodies associated with liberal democratic practice, doxxing sites such as Canary Mission serve as an escalating threat to many scholars. Indeed, ICE and the US State

Department are acting to detain and deport students identified by Canary Mission and the American branch of the Zionist extremist organization Betar.[12]

In recent months I have heard a number of reports of Jewish academics listed on the Canary Mission site being targeted when trying to enter United States. There are some parallels here with the targeting of Jews during the McCarthy era. It is notable, here, that Jews opposed to Trump are in his sights—calling Chuck Schumer "not Jewish anymore" and "a Palestinian" is one obvious and bizarre example. False charges of antisemitism are being wielded by the right to crush even those slightly to the left of centre.

But the real threat, clearly, is the broader global solidarity movement for Palestine. That solidarity movement threatens, arguably, not only Israel but contemporary settler colonial regimes (and ultimately global imperialism) everywhere. These include, significantly, in both so-called Canada and the United States where movements calling for *land back* to Indigenous peoples have grown increasingly strong over the past decade. There are important implications in this struggle for the history of the Jewish people and for antisemitism in Europe where Jewish settlement and landowning were prohibited or heavily restricted. Jews under the Russian Empire, for example, were confined to the "Pale of Settlement," a region alluded to in the title of this collective essay.

There is currently an understanding that the singularity of this conflict—particularly, unwavering American support, including for war crimes, and its rejection of international bodies such as the UN and the ICC—

has eroded global trust in liberal democracy, among other things. Is there a parallel for this in academia? What will be the lasting legacy of the treatment of the encampments and the punishment of students and faculty for their support of Palestine?

ANNA ZALIK: These echoes to earlier periods in the midst of a genocidal war on Palestine purportedly in the defense of "Jewish safety" have prompted many of us to increasingly ponder the historical legacy of the so-called "Jewish left," including its relationship to Zionism.

Inspired by the historian A.R. Takriti, over the past year I turned to the writings of Winston Churchill, who strongly supported the Zionist movement in the interwar years of the 20th century. I was stunned, given the pro-Israel and pro-British information I have been surrounded by throughout most of my life, to discover that Churchill was clearly antisemitic.[13] This is particularly apparent in a little-known column he wrote in 1920 entitled "Zionism vs. Bolshevism: A Struggle for the Soul of the Jewish People."[14] The pro-Israel Canadian Jewish community indicates surprise at the fact that Churchill was both an antisemite and a Zionist. Yet association of antisemitism with right-wing Zionism clearly dates back well over a century.

This relationship cannot be attended to in any historical detail here. But I raise it to note the way in which Zionism was used by imperial forces to dilute the role the Jewish left played in the early 20th century in support of revolutionary change in Europe and the Americas. Indeed, the Zionist movement's ultimate success in creating a Jewish state in Palestine greatly fractured the Jewish left in many parts of the world, including in Palestine itself where the Jews in the Palestinian Communist Party threw in their lot with the newly created state of Israel in 1948.[15] If nothing else, the reawakening of the Jewish left to this suppressed part of our history at this pivotal and horrifying moment of Israel's genocidal campaign in Gaza, the reawakening of the Jewish left to this suppressed part of our history may help us gain the moral clarity and historical understanding to reflect upon, critique and revive our role in broader struggles for justice and emancipation.

Notes

1. Arms Embargo Now, "Exposing Canadian Military Exports," *Palestinian Youth Movement* and World Beyond War, 29 July 2025.
2. Robert Brym, Jews and Israel 2024 Survey: Ten Further Insights, *Canadian Jewish Studies*, 30 May 2024.
3. York University Race Equity Committee. *Surveilled & Silenced: A Report on Palestine Solidarity at York University*. 3 October 2024.
4. Laurie E. Adkin, *Unjustified: The Kent report's exoneration of the violation of protestors' Charter rights at the University of Alberta in May 2024*, 18 March 2025.
5. York Federation of Students, "Statement on Morning Encampment Raid at York University," *The Bullet*, 6 June 2024. /
6. York Professors for Palestine, "York Faculty Letter Denouncing Police Raid on York Popular University for Palestine: Open Letter to President Lenton and the York University Board of Governors."
7. See this volume, "Policing the Window: The Case of the Indigo 11", Thoby King.
8. Committee on Academic Freedom, Middle East Studies Association of North America, "Exposing Canary Mission: A Resource for College and University Leaders."
9. Jonah Corne, Shiri Pasternak, "On CBC media capitulation and HonestReporting Canada," *Canadian Dimension*, 27 May 2024.
10. "YUACRI members respond to suspension in open letter," YUFA, 4 April 2027.
11. York University Advisory Committee on Responsible Investment, "Research and Recommendations on the YU Divest Proposal," March 2018.

12. Stephanie Saul, "A Mysterious Group Says Its Mission Is to Expose Antisemitic Students," *New York Times*, 1 April 2025.
13. Michael McMenamin, "Churchill and the 'Protocols of the Elders of Zion,'" The Churchill Project, 8 November 2021.
14. Winston Churchill, "Zionism vs. Bolshevism," 1920. Available on Wikisource.org.
15. Dorothy M. Zellner, "What We Did: How the Jewish Communist Left Failed the Palestinian Cause," *Jewish Currents*, 12 May 2021.

Duha Elmardi co-hosting a Community
Benefit for Sudan, Montreal, April 2025.
Photo: Leila Marshy

CHAPTER 17

A Sudan and Palestine: Resisting Erasure in the Attention Economy

Duha Elmardi

On a May afternoon in 2024, Sudanese and other Black students, scholars, and allies gathered at the McGill University student encampments to commemorate the connections between Palestine, Sudan, and Black resistance. The speakers, primarily Sudanese and non-Sudanese Black people and members of the Sudan Solidarity Collective, discussed how the struggles of Palestine, Sudan, and Black people were intertwined as global struggles against colonialism and capitalism. Through poetry, banner making, discussions, and some tears, we shared reflections on what showing up for Sudan and for each other can look like. A few days earlier, I joined a reading circle at the McGill encampment, where Black students shared lessons on George Jackson's life and legacy. Both of these experiences felt like the embodiment of what Fannie Lou Hamer described in her famous speech, "Nobody's Free Until Everybody's Free."

I am writing this essay on the 701st day of the genocide in Gaza and on the 875th day since the SAF-RSF war in Sudan began. The counterrevolutionary[1] war in Sudan has devastated every aspect of life, especially for those unable to leave. Countless lives have been lost, whether by missiles and aerial bombardments, by stray bullets, or in accidents while trying to evacuate. Others have died of dehydration or starvation. Diseases such as dengue fever, malaria, and cholera have spread rapidly with the collapse of Sudan's healthcare system.[2] And then there are those who have died suddenly from heart attacks and the crushing weight of grief.

Over 14 million Sudanese people have been forced from their homes and regions, making it the largest displacement crisis in the world. Currently, residents in Al Fashir, the capital of the state of North Darfur, have been under siege by the Rapid Support Forces (RSF) for more than 500 days, with all supplies being blocked from entry. Along with several other areas in Sudan, Al Fashir has hit a stage five famine phase according to the standards of the Integrated Food Security classification (IPC).[3] Many in the Darfur region are survivors of the state-sanctioned genocide that was committed in the early 2000s jointly with the Janjaweed militias prior to their rebranding as the RSF. Hundreds of thousands of people have since endured multiple waves of displacement, ethnic cleansing, and other violence.

As in Palestine, many have noted that the war in Sudan is the result of a convergence of global capital interests, neoliberal policies, and inherited British colonial legacies. Militarized and political actions over the decades have marginalized millions of Sudanese in Darfur, the Nuba

Mountains, Blue Nile State, and parts of Eastern Sudan. The story of Sudan has been simplified and weaponized with binaries such as Muslim and Non-Muslim, African and Arab, Native and Non-native. Tribal hierarchies are exploited in geopolitical games that extend beyond its borders. Land[4], gold[5], and other resources are at the heart of this struggle, as the United Arab Emirates, Egypt, Israel, the US, and other states have each been involved with one or another of the warring factions or in counterrevolutionary efforts at large.

In spite of the fact that in January 2025, it was officially determined by the US State Department that what was happening in Sudan was a genocide,[6] the United States has repeatedly used Sudan as a pawn in its complicity and funding of genocide in Palestine. In his confirmation hearing that same month, US state secretary Marco Rubio called Sudan a "real genocide" while warning other countries from recognizing Palestine. Most recently, the Trump administration has named Sudan as a possible relocation destination for Gazans threatened with removal from their homelands. This has been rejected by Sudanese officials. Meanwhile, the US government continues to supply its ally, the United Arab Emirates, with military weapons in spite of its role in the conflict in Sudan.

There is even a local connection. I am in the same city where the Sudanese community protested Dickens & Madson, a Montreal-based Canadian PR firm run by lobbyist and former Israeli military intelligence member, Ari Ben-Menashe. In 2019, shortly before the brutal crackdown on the 58-day Khartoum sit-in attended by millions, known as the Khartoum massacre,[7] Dickens & Madson signed a $6M deal with the Sudanese transitional military to enhance their image and establish connections with the US, Russia, and other countries.[8] They also helped to arrange a meeting between RSF leader Mohamed Hamdan Daggalo and US President Donald Trump.

In Canada, repression related to Sudan manifests as invisibilization, anti-Blackness, and institutionalized neglect. Media outlets barely cover the war or the struggles faced by Sudanese people in Canada; mainstream journalists reject coverage requests; and racist remarks from politicians and elected members are common. Recently, in a private meeting with the Sudanese community in Montreal, a Canadian MP felt comfortable enough to tell them that Canada must be cautious because the Sudanese people "bring diseases".

The Sudanese community in Canada has consistently voiced its concerns about the discriminatory and abysmal nature of immigration programs and policies, including their inaccessible financial requirements.[9] As with the immigration program for Gazans, applicants have died while waiting for their papers to be processed,[10] leaving families and refugees in limbo with little communication or care. In February 2025, the Canadian government committed to accepting only 4,000 government-assisted Sudanese refugees, but most applicants have still not arrived. When we examine the precedent set by the Ukraine emergency program—accessible to all Ukrainians regardless of family ties in Canada; no application fees; no financial requirements; a brief 14-day processing schedule; and *almost one million visas approved*—it is evident that the Canadian response to Sudan is structural discrimination and anti-Black racism.

I write this essay from the vicinity of Montreal's Concordia University, where I was a graduate student during the first year of the current war in Sudan. The lack of institutional support for Sudanese students or recognition of their situation was telling. However, this came as no surprise. Despite publicly apologizing for its role during the 1969 Sir George Williams campus student protests and establishing an anti-Blackness task force in 2020 after the murder of George Floyd and the subsequent protests for Black lives,[11] Concordia University continues to both ignore Sudanese protests and repress those who speak out against Israeli genocide, including calls for divestment.

Repression regarding Palestine and the neglect of Sudan are not unique to Concordia. During an alternative "people's" graduation at the University of Toronto, Sudanese educator and writer Dr. Nisrin Elamin noted that, in a meeting where she advocated for support for Sudanese students in this time of crisis, the university admitted that its policies "mirrored the Canadian state," therefore, Sudanese students would receive no meaningful support from the administration.

> We left the meeting empty-handed that day, with no commitments or accommodations. Instead, this administrator gifted us the analytical framework for understanding the relationship between our university and the settler-colonial state in and beyond North America...in their refusal to divest from genocide and in their deliberate prioritization of profit over student demands and well-being.[12]

This imposed scarcity trickles down into community and activist spaces. When attempts are made to broaden Palestine anti-colonial discourse to include actions in solidarity with Sudan, Congo, Haiti, Tigray or other struggles, a resistance manifests in the form of invisibilization, neglect and anti-Blackness. These attempts are seen as taking attention away from Palestine, are considered unimportant, secondary and divisive, and are shut down. However, one is expected to mention Palestine when discussing Sudan, the Congo, or other places, even when a comparison isn't needed.

I can recount many hours of debriefing and unpacking that my Sudanese comrades and I do in private after participating in solidarity actions and being subjected to erasure and anti-Blackness. But discussing this on a larger level is difficult and daunting.

And then there are the Zionists and right-wing influencers who use Sudan as a talking point to support their narrative, despite having never shown genuine concern for the country. Zionist propaganda of this type is intended to incite division and undermine solidarity, a perspective obvious to Sudanese individuals whenever they encounter it.

Combatting Zionism is the task of all peoples engaged in anti-colonial struggles. Our collective efforts are essential to this; however, we must also expand our capacity to have these difficult conversations within and between our movements.

Muzan Alneel, a Sudanese engineer, researcher, and public speaker, stated in her insightful article, "Failing Palestine by failing the Sudanese revolution," that the normalization of suffering removes struggles from their material context—making them about identity, religion, or cultural conflict rather than concrete issues of land, resources, and global geopolitical interests.[13] When movements are forced to compete for attention rather than building long-term revolutionary analysis, they become vulnerable to manipulation by forces that benefit from keeping oppressed populations divided and focused on symbolic rather than structural change.

Alneel demonstrates how mainstream media's "breaking news" model pits different crises against each other for airtime, creating artificial competition between causes like Sudan and Gaza. Citing one such news cycle, she writes: "Overnight, the Sudanese public witnessed a dramatic drop in the quality and quantity of updates on their homeland, to the extent that infrequent programmes dedicated to news about Sudan started to be advertised as coverage of a forgotten war."

The erasure of Sudan within Canadian institutions, the suppression of Palestinian solidarity movements, and the suppression of Sudanese protests within larger struggles all reflect a wider pattern through which universities, media, governments, and international actors uphold the priorities of the settler-colonial state. Genuine solidarity must not suffer from scarcity or be a competition for visibility; it must rest on the recognition that freedom and dignity are indivisible rights belonging to all oppressed peoples. Such solidarity requires attentiveness to the particularities of each struggle while remaining rooted in the shared task of imagining and building liberatory futures.

In Sudan and Palestine, those futures are already being forged: in the revolutionary charter of the Sudanese resistance committees; in the many forms of Palestinian steadfastness and resistance; in the refugee camps and schools that shelter the displaced; in the community kitchens and improvised clinics sustained by emergency response rooms; in the women's collectives resisting sexual violence; in the quiet strength of my mother and her neighbours, who held each other through unrelenting bombardment; in the Mohawk Warrior Society flag[14] carried through the hills and alleys of the occupied West Bank; and in the very soil marked by the blood of martyrs.

Notes

1. Sarah Abbas et al, "In Sudan, the People's Revolution Versus the Elite's Counterrevolution," Hammerandhope.org, Summer 2024.
2. "Sudan conflict leaves health system in near collapse: report," Sudan Tribune, 4 October 2023.
3. *Sudan: IPC Acute Food Insecurity Snapshot–October 2024 - May 2025*, ReliefWeb.int
4. "Land and power grabs in Sudan," GRAIN, 11 March 2025.
5. "Sudan's lead gold producer exporting direction to the 'enemy'," Ayin Network, 18 August 2024.
6. *Genocide Determination in Sudan and Imposing Accountability Measures*, Press Release, Antony Blinken, US Department of State, 7 January 2025.
7. "They were shouting 'Kill Them': Sudan's Violent Crackdown in Khartoum," Report, Human Rights Watch, 17 November 2019.
8. Andrew Russell, "Canadian firm inks $6M deal to push 'political aims' of Sudan's military regime," Global News, 28 June 2019.
9. Isha Bhargava, "Sudanese Canadians demand urgency from Ottawa almost 1 year after applying for family members to flee war," CBC News, 14 February 2025.
10. Shumaila Mubarak, "Sudanese Canadians fight to bring families out of war-torn Sudan," The New Arab, 5 September 2025.
11. Statement: Concordia's apology, President's Task Force on Anti-Black Racism, Concordia University, 28 October 2022.
12. Nisrin Elamin, "From Palestine to Sudan: Solidarity with Our Students," American Anthropologist.
13. Muzan Alneel, "Failing Palestine by failing the Sudanese revolution," Transnational Institute, 19 September 2024.
14. "Mohawk Warrior flag flies in Palestine," Mohawk Nation News, 1 June 2024.

PART FOUR

HEALTH CARE

CHAPTER 18

Statement: End the Repression in Canada's Health Sector

Health Workers Alliance for Palestine (HAP)

Since October 2023, Israel has implemented "a concerted policy to destroy the health-care system of Gaza."[1] Israel has targeted nearly every hospital in Gaza as part of its genocidal war; as of April 30, 2025, only 22 of Gaza's 35 hospitals remain partially functional, while 60 per cent of primary health centres have been destroyed.[2] To date, Israel's military has killed 1,200 Palestinian healthcare workers and 408 aid workers,[3] and it has abducted and tortured hundreds of healthcare workers, many of them specifically because they are healthcare workers.[4] Israeli physicians are accused of participating in this torture.[5] The toll of this genocide has reached horrific proportions: as of April 30, 2025, 52,400 Palestinians have been killed and 119,014 injured by Israel, and "it is not implausible to estimate that up to 186,000 or even more deaths could be attributable to the current conflict in Gaza."[6] Amidst unimaginable conditions, Gazan medical and public health personnel have worked steadfastly to preserve and honour life.

In opposition to these genocidal crimes and in solidarity with our courageous healthcare colleagues, scores of health workers of conscience across Canada and around the world have spoken out,[7] supported protest efforts including the Boycott, Divestment and Sanctions (BDS)[8] movement, and contributed directly to humanitarian relief missions in Gaza and Lebanon. Alarmingly, many of these health workers and learners have experienced a relentless, multi-pronged campaign of harassment, intimidation, and silencing, which treats Palestinians and speech in support of Palestinian rights as inherently antisemitic or sympathetic to terrorism. Simultaneously, there has been an inexcusable lack of accountability within Canadian health institutions for individuals[9] whose support for the state of Israel has taken the form of harassment and threats.[10] This is anti-Palestinian racism (APR),[11] and it has been leveled especially against Palestinian, Muslim, and Arab health workers, along with other racialized people and gender minorities. Despite widespread APR, these health workers and learners have continued to stand firm in support of justice.

Targeting of Palestinian Rights Defenders Is Not New

We have arrived at what the BC Civil Liberties Association calls "a watershed moment of peril for civil liberties in Canada."[12] But the targeting of Palestinian rights defenders is not new. As documented in the 2022 Independent Jewish Voices report, *Unveiling the Chilly Climate: The Suppression of Speech on Palestine in Canada*,[13] there has long been widespread APR in academia, including political interference in hiring practices, cancellation of events, harassment (including threatened and actual violence), and doxxing of Palestinian rights advocates. In 2021, for example, the International Human Rights Program at the University of Toronto rescinded a job offer to renowned legal scholar Valentina Azarova following donor interference which cited her record of work on Palestinian rights.[14] Notably, the donor was a board member of the Centre for Israel and Jewish Affairs (CIJA). This example of APR was an international scandal[15] and led to the censure of the university by the Canadian Association of University Teachers. Also in 2021, Dr. Ritika Goel, who at the time was the Faculty Lead in Social Accountability with the Department of Family and Community Medicine at the University of Toronto, faced accusations of antisemitism and calls for her dismissal after she posted to her personal social media account in support of Palestinians.[16] The campaign against Dr. Goel was promoted by the lobby group Friends of Simon Wiesenthal Center.[17]

These forms of repression and targeting[18] have only escalated alongside the escalating genocide, starvation, and destruction of health infrastructure in Gaza. This is occurring despite advocacy in support of Palestinian rights being in line with stated institutional goals of health equity and justice, and the growing body of evidence detailing Israel's violations of Palestinian rights. The International Criminal Court has issued arrest warrants for top Israeli officials. The International Court of Justice has issued an Advisory Opinion finding that Israel's policies and practices in the Occupied Palestinian Territory amount to apartheid.[19] And the world's leading human rights organizations have concluded that Israel is committing genocide against Palestinians in Gaza, including by using starvation and the deprivation of water as weapons of extermination.

Institutionalizing APR in Healthcare

Because of its status, healthcare represents an important platform from which pro-Israel advocacy groups in Canada attempt to legitimize the policies and actions of the state of Israel, and to smear and silence its critics. There are presently efforts within the health sector to institutionalize suppression of speech that is critical of the state of Israel.

The most prominent example of these efforts comes from the Canadian Federation of Jewish Medical Associations (CFJMA), an umbrella organization comprising the Jewish Medical Association of Ontario (JMAO), the Jewish Medical Association of British Columbia (JMABC), the Jewish Physicians Association of Manitoba, l'Association des Médecins Juifs du Québec (AMJQ), and similar groups that claim to represent the interests of Jewish physicians and medical learners. In reality, these groups have a political mission: building solidarity with Israel. The JMAO, for example, welcomes only Zionist Jewish members.[20] In its submission to Canada's Standing Committee on Justice and Human Rights in June 2024, the CFJMA calls for universities and their affiliated medical schools to adopt the International Holocaust Remembrance Alliance (IHRA) working definition of antisemitism as a "regulatory tool."[21] The IHRA definition has been widely[22] discredited[23] and rejected,[24] including by the Canadian Association of University Teachers and numerous Jewish organizations. The IHRA definition conflates criticism of the state of Israel with antisemitism, which weaponizes antisemitism to suppress speech on Palestine.

Examples of APR in Healthcare

Herein we present four cases—among countless others—of healthcare workers in Canada who have been targeted for speaking out for Palestinian rights and against the destruction of healthcare infrastructure in Gaza, including the targeted killing, disappearance, sexual abuse, rape, and torture of colleagues. These public cases illustrate a range of techniques used to target hundreds of health professionals and learners, including harassment, doxxing, censorship, baseless suspension, and, most consistently, the weaponization of a politicized definition of antisemitism.[25] Like many others, these individuals have refused to be silenced, and they continue to speak truth to power.

Case 1 – Dr. Ben Thomson: Suspension, Weaponization of Antisemitism, Doxxing, Threats

In October 2023, Dr. Thomson, a nephrologist at Mackenzie Richmond Hill Hospital who has done humanitarian medical work in Gaza, was suspended without pay following social media posts expressing support for Palestine.[26] Some of Dr. Thomson's posts warned against misinformation leading to the dehumanization of Palestinians and the justification of Israel's genocide. Dr. Thomson was smeared as antisemitic, and his home address was shared online. He received numerous death threats, which forced him to leave home under the advice of police, and his workplace received bomb threats. Given the lack of any grounds for suspension, Dr. Thomson was ultimately reinstated.[27]

Case 2 – Dr. Mathew Hannouche: Racism, Weaponization of Antisemitism, Complaints Against Learners

Dr. Hannouche, a critical care physician in Montreal, signed a letter published by Health Workers Alliance for Palestine on November 10, 2023, titled "Urgent Statement Against the Israeli Destruction of the Health System in Gaza."[28] The letter garnered more than 3,700 signatures from health workers across Canada. Dr. Hannouche did not promote the letter or reveal that he had signed it. Nevertheless, on November 13, 2023, he began receiving racist and defamatory emails from numerous colleagues, accusing him of antisemitism. Hospital leaders and physician colleagues were copied on these emails. In his written brief for the House of Commons Standing Committee on Justice and Human Rights in June 2024, Dr. Hannouche notes that he subsequently became aware that at least ten medical learners at McGill suffered "attacks, complaints or accusations of baseless antisemitism related to their advocacy for Palestinian human rights," adding, "[t]he learner in every case was Arab, and the majority were visibly Muslim women."[29]

Case 3 – Dr. Leslie Solomonian: Censorship, Weaponization of Antisemitism, Workplace Complaints

Dr. Solomonian is a naturopathic doctor and professor at the Canadian College of Naturopathic Medicine. In

January 2024, she responded to an Instagram post by the college marking the International Day of Holocaust Remembrance, which called for upholding human rights for all. Dr. Solomonian expressed agreement with this sentiment and drew attention to the unfolding genocide in Gaza. Later the same day, without consultation, her comment was removed. She subsequently received a slew of messages charging her with antisemitism.[30] Her manager submitted a formal complaint against her for her comment and for other social media activity in support of Palestinian liberation, suggesting that she was denying the Nazi holocaust by comparing it to the "conflict" in Palestine. The complaint was investigated and closed. Notably, Dr. Solomonian's union, CUPE, has adopted a BDS mandate and has opposed IHRA.[31]

Case 4 – Dr. Gem Newman: Censorship, Weaponization of Antisemitism, Donor Interference

In May 2024, Dr. Newman delivered the valedictory address to the graduating class of the Max Rady College of Medicine at the University of Manitoba. In his remarks, Dr. Newman encouraged his classmates to oppose settler colonialism both at home and abroad and to demand a ceasefire in Gaza, including an end to Israel's deliberate targeting of medical infrastructure.[32] The ceremony was livestreamed on YouTube and the university's website. However, the recording was removed after donor Ernest Rady wrote a letter to the university's president and its Faculty of Health Sciences dean, demanding that the valedictory remarks be cut. Rady's letter accused Dr. Newman of "hate speech" as well as "disrespect[ing] and disparag[ing] Jewish people as a whole, including Jewish students."[33] The Faculty of Health Sciences dean condemned the address, while the University of Manitoba Faculty Association president supported Dr. Newman's freedom of expression. Since beginning his residency, Dr. Newman has faced more than 20 complaints, many demanding that he not be permitted to practice medicine.[34] In April 2025, all complaints filed against Dr. Newman were resolved informally, with the College of Physicians and Surgeons of Manitoba finding no evidence of wrongdoing.

Across all of the cases above, we are not aware of any individual or institution having been held accountable for the vexatious accusations of antisemitism, the resultant impacts on professional reputation and livelihood, or the personal and legal financial costs. The refusal of Canada's shamefully silent health institutions to hold perpetrators of APR accountable emboldens attackers and signals implicit institutional endorsement of both the form and content of the attacks.[35]

Health Institutions Must Uphold Their Declared Commitments to Justice, Equity, and Human Rights

While Gaza's health system is systematically destroyed by Israel, health workers in Canada who protest the bombing of hospitals and the killing of colleagues in Gaza face silencing, harassment, bullying, and the risk of dismissal from our workplaces. As we expose this repression and its harms, we proudly reaffirm our principled stance in support of Palestinian rights and unequivocally declare that this repression will only motivate us to speak louder. We will not be silenced.

Upholding institutional mandates for health equity and justice demands that the targeting of those who speak out for Palestinian rights must end. Terms that describe Palestinian life under occupation and the Palestinian struggle for self-determination, such as *apartheid,*[36] *settler colonialism,*[37] *ethnic cleansing,*[38] *genocide,*[39] and *From the River to the Sea*[40] must not be censored. Discussion around and support for the BDS movement must be permitted, and critiques[41] of the political ideology of Zionism, including claims[42] that it is a racist ideology, must not result in censure.

We therefore expect:

1. That our rights to free speech and academic freedom are protected, especially as they relate to advocacy for Palestinian rights, including the right to self-determination.
2. That health faculties and institutions reject the IHRA definition of antisemitism.
3. That health faculties and institutions hold accountable members who commit—or have committed—acts of anti-Palestinian racism.
4. An end to interference by pro-Israel lobby groups in institutional decision making.

Endorsed by:

Ontario Council of Hospital Unions/Canadian Union of Public Employees (OCHU-CUPE)
Arab Canadian Lawyers Association (ACLA)
International Centre of Justice for Palestinians (ICJP) – Canada
Independent Jewish Voices Canada (IJV)
Doctors Against Genocide (DAG)
Palestinian Youth Movement (PYM)

Faculty for Palestine (F4P)
Labour for Palestine (L4P)
Palestinian Feminist Collective
Canadians for Justice and Peace in the Middle East (CJPME)
Canadian Muslim Healthcare Network (CMHN)
Canadian Muslim Public Affairs Council (CMPAC)
Jewish Faculty Network (JFN) Steering Committee
United Jewish People's Order Canada (UJPO)
Jews Say No to Genocide Coalition
Steering Committee of the Hearing Palestine Initiative at the University of Toronto
BC Nurses United for Social Justice
BC Doctors Against Genocide
Médecins du Québec Contre Le Génocide à Gaza
Pivot Legal Society
United for Peace – Canadian Interfaith Coalition
Toronto Indigenous Harm Reduction
Ottawa Healthcare Professionals for Palestine
Vancouver Healthcare Workers for Palestine
Canadians in Support for Refugees in Dire Need (CSRDN)
Independent Jewish Voices Toronto–York Region
Health Providers Against Poverty (HPAP)
Coordinating Council 4 Palestine (CC4P)
Science for the People Canada

Notes

1. "Report of the Independent International Commission of Inquiry on the Occupied Palestinian Territory, including East Jerusalem, and Israel," United Nations General Assembly, Seventy-ninth session, Item 71. 11 September 2024.
2. Unless otherwise indicated, all numbers quoted in this statement are from the United Nations Office for the Coordination of Humanitarian Affairs, "Reported impact snapshot, Gaza Strip," 30 April 2025.
3. "Palestinian aid workers likely shot execution style, forensic expert says," *Al Jazeera*, 4 April 2025.
4. *Palestinian Healthcare Workers Tortured*, Report. Human Rights Watch, 26 August 2024.
5. Owen Dyer, "Israeli doctors participated in torture, alleges released director of al-Shifa Hospital," *BMJ*, 286, 19 July 2024.
6. Rasha Khatib, Martin McKee, Salim Yusuf, "Counting the dead in Gaza: difficult but essential," *The Lancet*, Volume 404, Issue 10449, P2370238, 20 July 2024.
7. "Healthcare Workers as Human Rights Defenders: A Medical Perspective on Israel's Genocide enablement apparatus in Gaza and Abroad," The United Nations Special Rapporteur for the Right to Health, 10 January 2025.
8. See Appendix, BDS.
9. Allie Moustakis, "Queen's Medical School professor under investigation after complaints of anti-Palestinian racism," the *Queen's University Journal*, 24 January 2025.
10. Dr. Thea Weissdorf, "I hope you never need healthcare from UofT, she says, You guys wouldn't live very long." As reported by Samira Mohyeddin on *X*, 16 June 2024.
11. Dania Majid, "Anti-Palestinian Racism: Naming, Framing and Manifestations," report prepared for the Arab Canadian Lawyers Association, 25 April 2022.
12. "BCCLA Statement Against the Systemic Suppression of Support for Palestine," British Columbia Civil Liberties Association, 13 March 2025.
13. Sheryl Nestel, Rowan Gaudet, "Unveiling the Chilly Climate: The Suppression of Speech on Palestine in Canada," Independent Jewish Voices, 12 October 2022.
14. Shanifa Nasser, "Censure against U of T temporarily suspended after school reverses course in hiring controversy," *CBC News*, 17 September 2021.
15. Masha Gessen, "Did a University of Toronto Donor Block the Hiring of a Scholar for Her Writing on Palestine?" *The New Yorker*, 8 May 2021.

16. Nick Boisvert, "Supporters of U of T doctor describe allegations of antisemitism as 'disingenuous' and stifling," *CBC News*, 29 May 2021.
17. "FSWC Calls for Action by U of T Administration as Jewish Medical Students Report Antisemitism, Intimidation, Harassment," Media Release, Friends of Simon Wiesenthal Center, 21 May 2021.
18. Brishti Basu, "Abuse of power: Hospitals, med schools crack down on Palestine advocacy," *The Breach*, 29 February 2024.
19. "Summary of the Advisory Opinion," International Court of Justice, Document number 186-20240719-SUM-01-00-EN, 19 July 2024.
20. "[The] JMAO supports the right of Jews to self-determination, considers Israel to be the ancestral homeland of the Jewish people, believes in the right of Jews to act as a people, and supports the right of the State of Israel to exist. This is what we mean by "Zionism"—a term we use with purpose and pride. JMAO opposes any effort to dismantle or eliminate the State of Israel...Criticism of Israel that rises to the level of antisemitism as determined by the IHRA Working Definition will not be tolerated." FAQ, Jewish Medical Association of Ontario.
21. Lisa Salamon, Submitted on behalf of the Canadian Federation of Jewish Medical Associations.
22. "128 scholars warn: Don't trap the United Nations in a vague and weaponized definition of antisemitism," EUObserver, 3 November 2022.
23. Chris McGreal, "UN urged to reject antisemitism definition over 'misuse' to shield Israel," *The Guardian*, 24 April 2023.
24. Institutional Rejections of the IHRA Definition, List, NOIHRA.org
25. Daniel Rosenbaum, Samantha Green, Michaela Beder, "Opinion: New Survey Exaggerates Antisemitic Threat in Medicine to Push IHRA, Stifling Criticism of Israel," *The Grind Magazine*, 22 December 2024.
26. Brishti Basu, "Ontario doctor suspended, his address published after pro-Palestinian social media posts," *CBC News*, 20 October 2023.
27. *Reinstatement of Dr Be Thomson by Mackenzie Health*, Statement, CJPME, 13 October 2023.
28. "Urgent Statement Against the Israeli Destruction of the Health System in Gaza," Health Workers Alliance for Palestine, 10 November 2023.
29. Brief Submitted to the Standing Committee on Justice and Human Rights, House of Commons. Presented by Matthew Hannouche, MD, Assistant Professor of Medicine, McGill University, Montreal, 21 June 2024.
30. Dr. Leslie Solomonian, professor, Canadian College of Naturopathic Medicine, Submission to the Standing Committee on Justice and Human Rights Re: Study of Antisemitism, 7 June 2024.
31. "Speaking up for freedom of speech and human rights everywhere: CUPE Ontario's Statement on Bill 168," CUPE-SCFP.

32. Dr. Gem Newman, Instagram, 16 May 2024.
33. Nicole Buffie, "Philanthropist who gifted $30M to U of M med school 'appalled' by valedictorian's 'hateful lies,'" *Winnipeg Free Press*, 21 May 2024.
34. Candice Bodnaruk, "Dr. Gem Newman Faces Attack for His Advocacy for Palestine," *Washington Report*, 20 January 2025.
35. Kavita Algu, "The Canadian medical establishment should not remain silent as Israel attacks Palestinian health care facilities," *Toronto Star*, 1 December 2024.
36. A regime of Jewish supremacy from the Jordan River to the Mediterranean Sea: This is apartheid. Report, B'Tselem, 12 January 2021.
37. Francesca Albanese, *Genocide as colonial erasure. Report of the Special Rapporteur on the situation of human rights in the Palestinian territories since 1967.* Report, United Nations, 1 October 2024.
38. "UN expert warns of new instance of mass ethnic cleansing of Palestinians, calls for immediate ceasefire," Press release, United Nations Human Rights Office of the Commissioner, 14 October 2023.
39. "Amnesty International investigation concludes Israel is committing genocide against Palestinians in Gaza," Amnesty International, 5 December 2024.
40. "From the River to the Sea: A Primer on History, Context, and Legalities in Canada," Hearing Palestine Initiative, University of Toronto, 2023.
41. IJV Statement on Zionism, Independent Jewish Voices, 12 November 2024.
42. Zvi Bar'el, "Zionism is Racism," *Haaretz*, 27 December 2022.

CHAPTER 19

What is Public Safety?

Katherine Grzejszczak

LEILA MARSHY: Can you tell us a little bit about yourself?

In the early 2000s, I was an undergraduate in Sociology but I didn't necessarily want to go to grad school. I was worried about job prospects—I could see that the jobs that were generally available in the private sector for an undergraduate degree were entry-level jobs, and that didn't really interest me. A friend of mine happened to be doing the paramedic program and convinced me at the time that it was a good idea. I had never thought about working in healthcare. I had only a few credits left for my undergraduate degree, but I dropped it and ended up enrolling in the paramedic program. I just fell in love with the job from day one.

From the time I began until very recently, my employer was York Region municipality, in the Greater Toronto Area, and I worked on a frontline ambulance. I was looking forward to continuing training so I could assume advanced care responsibilities. I was also active in the union, and am past-president of our Local 905.

And at what point did you start advocating for Gaza and Palestine? Is this a new awareness or part of something more longstanding?
I've always been aware and active. When I was at UofT doing my undergrad in the early 2000s, I was involved in the organizing against the Iraq war. Shortly after that, I began doing Palestinian solidarity work.

In June of this year, you were suddenly fired. What happened?
The context is that CUPE-ON (Canadian Union of Public Employees, Ontario branch) was organizing a Hands Off Iran rally to boycott the bombings. There was a Facebook events page and lots of online discussion. It was a controversial event and the union was being attacked online and in the *National Post*[1] for the rally. Fred Hahn, president of CUPE-ON, was particularly smeared in the media. And so, as a sitting member of the executive board, I posted a comment as part of a longer discussion thread. I defended the rally and thanked the union for organizing it.

> In the last 2 years Israel has bombed Palestine, Yemen, Lebanon, Syria and now Iran. They have been occupying Palestine for 75+ years. They are luring starving Palestinian children to their concentration camp food aid depots so they can snipe them dead. They keep murdering workers—media, healthcare, municipal—they just mass murdered 15 first responders, including 7 paramedics. Any union or other organization that doesn't fight this is choosing to stay silent during genocide. Thanks CUPE Ontario and Toronto & York Region Labour Council for asking members to join these demonstrations, to stop the bombing of Iran, You're one of the few who stand in solidarity with workers.

I based my words on corroborated facts. Regarding sniping, for example, there is ample physician testimony about treating Palestinian children with injury patterns of single gunshot wounds to the head and chest. Children do not accidently end up with bullets in their vital organs. These are the intentional acts of an occupying army.

What happened next?

That comment went up at approximately 1 am on Thursday, June 19. By 5 pm the next day, June 20, after a very short meeting where I was asked very few questions and had no opportunity for discussion, I was terminated. They didn't even give me anything in writing, no termination letter, because they said they didn't have one ready.

On Saturday morning the 21st of June, Dahlia Kurtz, who is a self-described Zionist activist, tweeted my comment and my picture and asked "Would you feel safe if this paramedic treated you?" This was followed by a celebratory tweet on June 22: "We did it! The keffiyeh paramedic was fired."

Then, also on the 22nd, municipal councillor Gila Martow seemed to admit that she was involved in my termination. In a Facebook post she wrote, "On Friday June 20 I was made aware of a paramedic employed by York Region who had allegedly posted a hateful message on social media. Vaughan Mayor Steven Del Duca immediately reached out to the Chair of York Region with the community's concerns. The matter was investigated and we have received confirmation that the individual is no longer employed by York Region."

While it's impossible to say how politically motivated my termination was, the speed of these posts indicates pretty clearly that a concerted effort was putting both pressure and influence on my employer. Due process has been completely absent. This had very little to do with safety or a question of my competence.

Was this the first time something like this happened to you?

In 2021, our union local passed a resolution to send a letter to the federal government asking for an arms embargo with Israel. Many union locals were passing similar resolutions at the time. We got quite a bit of pushback, but it didn't have its desired effect.

Then in April 2024, I was attacked for wearing a keffiyah and there was pressure on the union to remove me from the executive. Again, it didn't have the desired effect.

What is next?

The Union is pursuing my employer through a grievance and arbitration process. We've already had a couple of meetings. This will be a long process, months or even years.

Do you regret being so vocal about Palestine? You've lost a job you love.

I don't regret it at all. It is important for people to be speaking about genocide and organizing resistance and making demands, whether or not we may have to pay a cost. I loved my job and I want to return.

But as a healthcare worker, how can I not have this response to what is going on in Gaza? It was only four months ago that 15 emergency medical workers, including eight paramedics, were targeted and killed. Their bodies and vehicle were recovered days later in a mass grave of sand. They were murdered for trying to provide emergency medical care to wounded Gazans. The number of healthcare workers killed and hospitals bombed is unconscionable. I'm not aware of any ambulance service in the GTA or in Ontario who has said a single word to express any grief for fellow Red Crescent paramedics, let alone to condemn these war crimes.

Meanwhile, we are punishing and criminalizing those who are trying to throw a wrench in a war machine. A war machine that has annihilated over 60,000 people and shows no sign of stopping.

My comments on social media were labelled hateful. But what is hateful are the actions of the Israeli state towards Palestinians, not my descriptions of them. I love my job as a paramedic because it is first and foremost about preserving life and alleviating suffering. Organizing against a genocide is not a contradiction of those obligations, it is an extension of those professional obligations.

Seeking to end a genocide is not a threat to public safety, it *is* public safety.

Note

1. Ari David Blaff, "CUPE Ontario sponsoring 'Hands off Iran' rally outside US consulate this Sunday," *National Post*, 17 June 2025.

Dr. Yipeng Ge with Dr. Fozia Alvi (Founder and Chair of Humanity Auxilium) in Rafah, Gaza, while on a medical relief mission in February 2024.

CHAPTER 20

Two Letters

Yipeng Ge

After his suspension from the University of Ottawa for pro-Palestinian posts in early 2024, the Canadian physician refused to return to his residency. Instead, he went to Gaza. A year later, Dr Ge joined thousands from around the world at the Rafah border to attempt to break the siege.

Reflecting on the past 18 months of this ongoing genocide in Gaza, it feels like there is so much to still say and also so much already said. What is there left to say? In revisiting some moments in what I have witnessed and experienced from Turtle Island to Palestine, I want to share these two love letters to Palestine and to the students of conscience. Resistance is the deepest form of love. May we all continue to find the ways necessary to resist and persist in a struggle for a free and liberated Palestine.

In solidarity,
Yipeng Ge
March 2025

A love letter to Palestine[1]

Today, I am speaking from the unceded and unsurrendered territory of the Algonquin Anishinaabeg. I learned about allyship and solidarity work when I learned about the genocide of Indigenous peoples here on occupied Turtle Island from Haudenosaunee scholars and community members. Canada as a settler colonial state is made up of broken treaties and lands stolen from Indigenous peoples (First Nations, Inuit, Metis). For me, spending time with Indigenous communities, whether it be at Six Nations of the Grand River or in Nunavut in the North, I learned that resistance to colonial violence and erasure takes many forms.

Resistance in Palestine by Palestinians against genocidal colonial violence and erasure also takes many forms. Not only is resistance the deepest form of love, but it is rooted in preservation of dignity, life, care, and ultimately justice. Palestinians, Indigenous to their territory, find themselves resisting colonization and extermination because it is necessary to protect and preserve their people and their community on their traditional lands, which have been occupied for generations since before the ongoing Nakba, or "catastrophe," began in 1948.

As a non-Palestinian, I am privileged and grateful to have visited Palestine and to have shared many beautiful memories with amazing people. I have fond memories of visiting places like Nablus in the West Bank to try their famous knafeh, a traditional pastry dessert made with cheese soaked in syrup and topped with pistachios. Or hiking in Battir, walking amongst a landscape of olive trees, grapevines, stone terraces, poppies, and other flowers. Learning about the ancient irrigation system, one of the oldest farming methods, which remains a source of livelihood for local Palestinian communities. Or watching a Dabke performance and later even attempting to learn the traditional Palestinian dance.

I have learned from Indigenous communities here on Turtle Island and from Palestinians in Palestine that your stories, your histories, your food, your art, your music, your dance, your culture, your language, your joy—they are all forms of resistance against colonial violence and erasure.

One of the most pertinent examples was from my time in Gaza earlier this year in the midst of ongoing overt genocide. There were a handful of occasions where I saw kites being flown by children. These kites varied in their construction. Some appeared to have been made with materials like plastic or garbage bags, but they worked well and they were beautiful to see flying in the sky. Against a backdrop of drones, quadcopters, fighter jets, and ongoing shelling, to see a kite in the sky now and then showed me the steadfastness of the Palestinian people and children that I simply can't put into words. The only hot meals I ate in Gaza were because the Palestinian healthcare workers demanded that we share meals together. Knowing they had so little, they still wanted to do more for us as their guests—I left my heart in Gaza.

I realize now that this is a love letter to Palestine.

Ultimately, Palestinians in Palestine will liberate themselves through their resistance efforts on the ground. But that does not absolve us from the moral obligation and legal responsibility to end Canada's complicity, support, and active involvement in Israel's ongoing apartheid and genocide of the Palestinian people. We have a duty to the Palestinian people to do what we can from where we are, through meaningful, intersectional, and unwavering solidarity, to support their efforts towards self-determination and liberation.

We must see recognition of a Palestinian state. We must see a permanent two-way arms embargo with Israel. We must see Canada comply with all of the ICJ rulings and the ICC arrest warrants. We must see unrestricted humanitarian aid for Gaza. We must see reparations for Palestinians. We must see an end to the illegal Israeli occupation of Palestine. We will see, within our lifetimes, Palestinians living free, and with their right of return honoured and fulfilled.

A love letter to the students of conscience[2]

This is a love letter to the students and to the community members who supported and nourished the student encampment. You put your heart, body, and soul into it. It was challenging work. You did it for a just and decent cause. You should be proud of what you have achieved.

For over 10 weeks, you persisted through rain and shine. For over 70 days, you held your ground. You demonstrated what it means to act on what you know to be true and right, to practice and exercise solidarity as an act of moral clarity. You are the best of us.

It was really special what you were able to build and co-create with one another. There was and still will be much learning from it all. Through the sacrifices, struggle, and imperfections, there remains so much beauty in what you have made possible.

It has been an honour to share time and space with you all in a place that was created on shared principles and values for human rights and liberation from structural oppression. May you take time to rest and sustain yourselves for the lifelong struggle of liberation for all.

A shared collective movement for the liberation of Palestinians and their right to self-determination on their traditional homelands brought us together. We demand an end to the complicity of the University of Ottawa as an academic institution that funds and supports genocide by Israeli forces.

It has become crystal clear that the University of Ottawa would rather spend money on dismantling an encampment than divesting from genocide and apartheid. But it will continue to be more costly to support war crimes, economically and morally. The tides are turning. Gaza is freeing us in this way.

Academic institutions have no place supporting crimes against humanity and funding the military-industrial complex that fuels the economy of war. You are more principled than so many so-called "leaders" that have done nothing but cower behind their institutional privilege.

The exercise and practice of leadership and solidarity is what you have shown us all in times of profound suffering and loss. It is an act of deep love and compassion for humanity. It has not gone unnoticed by so many, including the colleagues and friends I have made from Gaza.

You have successfully moved so many towards the hard truth. History is on your side. Justice is on your side. Standing with the oppressed comes with backlash. You have handled it all with grace, humility, and patience. Institutions are not immovable.

The heavy-handed tactics and repression by institutions in the form of disproportionate discipline, reprimands, or even suspensions and expulsions reflect their commitment to maintaining systemic oppression and anti-Palestinian racism. They do this to sow fear hoping the students of conscience will back down. We must continue to organize and push as hard as we can, be louder than ever before, in support of health and human rights for Palestine and Palestinians. This is how we fight the suppression and silencing of speech.

Please know that I hold you in the highest regard. Spending time with you in the space you have created was inspiring, empowering, and uplifting despite the sorrows of reality. I am sad this chapter has closed, but many new chapters lie ahead. There is more work to be done.

Onwards shall we go collectively towards liberation for all, including Palestinians in Gaza. In historic Palestine, in Jerusalem, in the West Bank, in the diaspora around the world. For the right to return. For equal human rights. For self-determination. Within our lifetimes.

Notes

1. The original text was delivered on November 29, 2024, at Parliament Hill on the International Day of Solidarity with the Palestinian People. Some of the text has been revised for clarity.
2. The original text was shared on July 11, 2024, on social media following the decampment of the students. Some of the text has been revised for clarity and additions.

PART FIVE

ARTS AND MINDS

NOTHING JUSTIFIES GENOCIDE. CANADIAN GOV: SPEAK UP!

"What happened to Israeli citizens is horrific and unspeakable. But it doesn't justify the massacre and starving of an entire population. Genocide is not an answer to terrorism. Don't kill children as revenge."
Posted to Instagram, 16 October 2023

STOP BOMBING CHILDREN

"I never thought I'd have to turn off the comments on this simple post."
Posted to Instagram, 2 November 2023

CHAPTER 21

Drawing Conclusions

Elise Gravel

LEILA MARSHY: You are one of the most popular children's authors and illustrators in Quebec, and very well-known throughout Canada. Your career has not been without controversy, however. Your book on gender stereotypes, *Pink, Blue and You,* was banned in some US states and school boards. Your work promoting vaccines during the pandemic, for example, also caught some negative attention. Then October 7, 2023, happened and you experienced a whole other level of response and reaction. Can you talk about that?

Yes, it was very different. For the earlier controversies (transgender, queer youth, vaccines), these were issues that the right wing took up. I already knew that the right wing will say and do horrible things about anything that's slightly different. But I don't really care and it doesn't affect me or influence my world view. Of course, it is stressful to be attacked like that in public, and knowing that my books were banned was not a pleasant feeling. Then again, banning books is a great way to make people talk about a book! In the end, I always felt I was supporting groups of people and ideas that needed to be supported, so I took the backlash and reactions in stride. It never felt personal.

The reactions to my posts after October 7, 2023, however, were very different and much harder to take. These attacks came not just from the right wing, but from the mainstream and even the left. There was unrelenting violence in these attacks, including death threats. I mean, it has been depressing to know what people had to say about transgender and queer youth—but I was truly horrified to see how much people were defending the killing of children in Gaza.

I literally CAN'T shut up. It's an impossibility. Sorry.
Posted to Instagram, 10 November 2023

Posted to Instagram, 24 January 2024

Were these attacks coming from specific people or organizations?

Well, first we have to say that our government set the tone by not saying or doing anything. This gave the appearance of consensus to the idea that it's acceptable to kill Palestinians, and that "genocide" was a dirty word. There was a political indifference that spread over everything. This had repercussions for me and a lot of people.

I never went to the police, but I took screenshots. After a while I started blocking anyone who left a threatening comment, or who wanted to engage in justification for genocide. I also hired a lawyer, just in case. At first, I could only respond by not responding, not engaging. But now these comments are deleted and blocked immediately. I will not waste my time or my energy.

Eventually, we tracked many of the comments and discovered that a large portion were coming from Israel.

How did you respond to this stress?

During the controversies about my writing about transgender and LGBTQ youth, there were always a few people who told me to shut up. But suddenly the amount of people telling me to shut up and that I have no right to say anything skyrocketed. Well guess what, it made me want to talk about it even more. Also, I understood very early on that my work was serving an educational purpose.

Between the fake news, the propaganda, and our own media's lack of scrutiny, it was more critical than ever to make sure people were paying attention to the truth. Many of my readers and followers were not necessarily educated about Palestine. Each one of my posts repre-

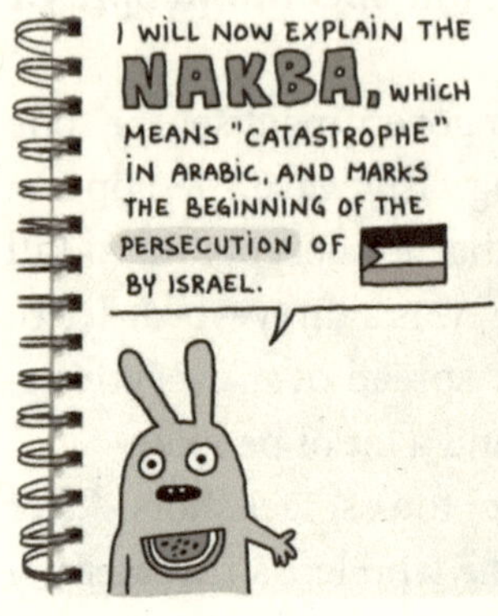

Here's an important word for those who are just starting their education on the tragedy. Posted to Instagram, 31 January 2024

sents a lot of research and reading and fact checking. In a way, we all learnt about this history of colonialism and occupation together.

Were you ever worried about damaging your reputation as a children's author, either with your readers or even your publishers?

For a long time, I was afraid of that happening, really scared about it in fact. People were cautious, telling me to stop and that it wasn't worth it. My publishers were being pressured to drop me, and at the very least they were encouraging me to step back from social media. One NYC publisher wrote me a letter asking whether I was aware that little Arab kids are taught to kill Jews. Well, she's not my publisher anymore. But my other publishers eventually saw the light and understood the broader situation, and they have stayed by me. In the end, I was not cancelled.

It's not a war, not a conflict.
It's a deliberate massacre.
Posted to Instagram,
26 January 2024

Posted to Instagram,
11 August 2025

You never shy away from using difficult and controversial words such as genocide or ceasefire or ethnic cleansing. Why is that important to you?
Because I see how our media and political leaders are always trying to frame the violence as a "war" or a "complicated conflict." In this way, the assumption is that the public can't possibly oppose Israel's actions. But it is crucial to call the violence by its real name. If what Hamas did was "terrorism," then Israel is doing something 100 times more violent. And you most certainly cannot call it "war."

You are always careful to distinguish your criticism of the Israeli state from that of the Jewish people in general. Can you talk about that?
I don't want to play Israel's game of associating its violent political settler movement to Judaism in general. Israel has created a system where any criticism of its political entity is seen as criticism of Judaism and the Jewish people. This rhetoric is political manipulation. Not only that, it puts Jews around the world at risk. Not to mention, I have many Jewish friends who do not support Zionism or Israel in any way. I always try to amplify these voices as well.

In February 2024, five months into the genocide, the Jewish Public Library responded to your outspokenness by removing your books from public access. In fact, I was part of a small group of people who spearheaded a petition against this. Within two days it was signed by hundreds of people, eventually adding to the pressure that forced the library to reinstate your books. Can you talk about what happened?
I can't speak to what motivated them, or what their logic was. Marc Cassivi was the first to write about it in *La Presse*,[1]

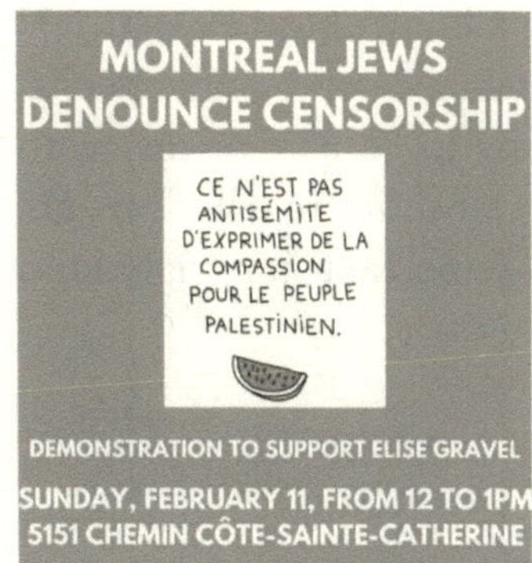

Yesterday, I was talking about solidarity and community. Today, my friends from @ voixjuivesmtl @ijvcanada are showing us what it means. Everyone is invited, Jews and non-Jews. Posted to Instagram, 10 February 2024

Thank you, merci, @voixjuivesmtl @ijvcanada for your support and solidarity. Posted to Instagram, 11 February 2024 Photo: No Borders Media

then every other media reached out to me for clarification and my take on it. It became not just a cause célèbre for me, but also a learning opportunity for everyone. Honestly, if the media hadn't given me the opportunity to talk about this, and if people hadn't responded the way they did, the dominant narrative would have been that I was antisemitic. I don't want to bash the library, though. They did what they thought was best, and when it was obvious that it wasn't, they changed course. The backlash to their action was very swift and very public, and their image was tarnished.

Has the Library ever reached out to you since then?
No, they have not.

Have you thought of writing a book about Palestine?
I have, but I would need to collaborate with someone, ideally a Palestinian. I'm happy to be part of the truth telling, but as a story it is not really mine to tell. There are a lot of people telling that very important story right now.

Montreal mural created by Elise Gravel
and Independent Jewish Voices, September 2024.

Note

1. Marc Cassivi, "Censure à la Bibliothèque publique juive de Montréal : *Une patate à l'index*", *La Presse*, 8 February 2024.

CHAPTER 22

How We Love: Protest as an Expression of Our Tenderness

Kagiso Lesego Molope

> Love is a powerful moral force on the side of justice.
>
> —Bernice King

PHOTO: X (Twitter)

On May 7, 2024, author Kagiso Lesego Molope was invited to the Politics and Pen Gala, a fundraiser hosted by the Writers' Trust of Canada. During the evening, Molope gave a speech where she spoke of the death toll and humanitarian cost of Israel's military campaign in Gaza. Her words were met with boos and heckles from the audience, and she was escorted out by security. The Writers' Trust later apologized for her treatment.

In my final year of undergraduate studies, I had an oral exam in which I had to speak "on progress and the role of the academy." I was studying literature and literary theory at the University of Cape Town, three years into the end of apartheid and the early days of democracy. This is South Africa's oldest university. It is one of the many universities known as "historically White institutions," words that serve as a reminder of who was there first, and who was and was not allowed in. I was the only Indigenous student in the class.

Constantly moving between two worlds has always been a struggle for me. In that class I wanted my two worlds to meet. In spite of the wealth of African literature in the country and the continent, I had never once been assigned an Indigenous writer in my classes. This grand institute that had existed for almost two centuries had only admitted its first Indigenous medical student in 1990—four years before apartheid was dismantled. I was exhausted by living in two worlds that never met. Struggling to keep track of where I could and could not speak my native language. Never referring to where I came from because my presence in that classroom didn't make sense for the professors, I was forever trying to prove that I was just like everyone around me.

There are things people see and things you have to work hard to hide. Like how loud your laugh is when you are at home. How your R is not rolled. The jokes you tell that are only funny in three African languages instead of one White language. That who you are is what you hide. And then there are the people you come from. What you feel for them and how they hold your authentic self. It is their love that pulled you through state violence: they hid you in their back rooms and gave you a wet cloth to hold over your face when tear gas first filled your lungs. You feel you can't make it through the rest of your life without them, so you bring them into rooms where casting them out is an unspoken requirement. This is what I did.

On the day of the exam, I stood in front of the professors and called attention to the glaring disconnect between the world of Indigenous people and the academy. I spoke of the university's lack of awareness of the living conditions outside of its borders. I said in order to remain relevant in a changing South Africa, the University of Cape Town had to acknowledge the world that exists outside its walls. A European education made little sense in an African country, I suggested. "We have to bring Africa into this institution." When I finished speaking, the examiner looked me in the eye, incredulous, and asked: "But aren't you grateful? Don't you feel *lucky* that you are in here, and they are out there?" He shook his head as if I were mad, and I'm sure to him that seemed the only explanation. I must have lost my mind to speak like this, to be standing inside the walls of the country's most prestigious university, one of the very select few of non-European students even allowed to be there, and be ungrateful for the opportunity!

My ingratitude earned me barely a pass. But I would not have changed my words. I had been loved back there, and that love was what had brought me into those centuries-old halls. How could I not speak for them, the ones outside the high walls of the university?

Decades later, I would have a similar interaction in a different setting.

On May 7th, 2024, seven months after Israel began its genocide on Palestinians, I was invited to a gala in Ottawa called Politics and the Pen. Ambassadors and members of parliament were invited along with a who's who list of authors to this night where the prestigious Shaughnessy Prize for Political Writing is awarded to a writer. It was my fourth year at the event. Every year I had enjoyed good conversation, great food, and met new people in the world of literature and politics.

But this was no ordinary year. Since the beginning of the war, I and most people I know had been attending marches and protests. We had been glued to our phones for updates from Gaza, wanting to keep up with the latest news. There were all the things that happen in wars, and more: starvation, displacement, torture, destruction of place and habitat. It was a livestreamed genocide and ethnic cleansing.

Everyone has their way of coping. Some people organize demonstrations. Others look for practical ways to be helpful. My particular way of feeling I had some grip on my sanity was to keep up with the numbers. Every morning, afternoon and just before going to bed I wrote down the death toll. I sought out the rate of the growing famine, the numbers of journalists and healthcare workers killed, the people on the ground who just disappeared.

Each day I counted current numbers and compared them to where they were the last time I had checked. It eventually became clear that the numbers reported were only a fraction of what was happening. Mass graves were being discovered. I know about mass graves. I come from a land of mass graves. No one can ever know for certain how many people are dying in any war.

So, I stopped counting. I ate too little or too much and then slept too little or too much. In the days leading up to the gala, I tried different coping strategies. In the mornings I'd turn my phone off, vowing I wouldn't look at it for the rest of the day. Then I swore I wouldn't look at it for the next six hours. Or five. Or two. Or the next thirty minutes.

Like everyone witnessing the horrors, I was losing my mind. Not only because we knew thousands were being killed every hour, but because while newspapers in the MENA (Middle East and North Africa) region and elsewhere in the Global South were reporting the genocide of Palestinians, in North American news, nothing like that was happening. The word genocide was not being used. There was no mention of Palestinians being killed, they only "died." In fact, there was hardly any mention of Palestinians at all. There was Israel and there was Hamas. It was an "Israel-Palestine war," a conflict between equals. The problem was not children being burnt alive or entire neighbourhoods eradicated. The problem, the only problem if you were only hearing it from Canadian newspapers, was that Hamas had taken Israeli hostages and Israel was under attack.

At the gala that evening, the wine was overflowing and the canapé trays were in circulation. It was a lovely, clear-sky evening and invited guests were in good form. I wanted to join in the fun so I made my own rules. I was going to enjoy the food. I would engage in the usual lively conversation with familiar faces. For a change I was not going to count how few Black people were there this year. I was not going to look at my phone and check *Al Jazeera*'s Live Tracker until I got home. But this is the problem with always living in two worlds that never meet: you are constantly on high alert. You train yourself to be in one place and forget the other. You change your behaviour, the opinions you express, the topics you engage in, and you learn to leave no trace of a second language on your tongue.

Like the European teachers in my historically White high school used to say: Leave the township at the door. Leaving yourself behind is a skill constantly required but one you never master. Not entirely.

After a while you feel as if you are going mad. You ask yourself whether you are the only one seeing the vastly different world outside the university—does the world outside the university even exist? If there is a famine and genocide taking place in another part of the world but we are happily in ball gowns and suits, with our media saying no such thing is happening, then are we perhaps imagining that there is a famine and genocide?

But then there is that ever-familiar nudge: the voices of people you care about still in your head. The lands that once held you demanding to be remembered. The feeling that if you say nothing you are choosing the rooms of power over these voices and these lands.

Looking around me, I panicked. In our blissfully ignorant, collective dream state, the old feeling of going mad resurfaced. Maybe there was no genocide? Just to be sure, I pulled out my phone and checked the numbers. *Al Jazeera* was reporting 35,287 Palestinians killed. The last time I'd checked, on April 18th, the day the invitation to the gala had come through my inbox, the numbers were at 23,357. Yes, there was a genocide and it was escalating. This being a gala celebrating politics and literature, I thought: What better place to speak on the war, to remind us that we had a humanitarian crisis beyond our borders? One that our government was actively supporting? Here was something that we might have the power to change, as a world superpower. As artists. The crisis was now a part of our collective history—one that some of us might even write about in the coming years.

So I thought: If you're going to say anything, you'd better quote facts. Getting the numbers exactly right was my only concern. I was amongst journalists and political experts. I didn't want to be accused of being wrong about facts. Paralyzing self-doubt is a thing that plagues every outsider. The notion that we can't ever be wrong if we are going to speak means we are in a perpetual state of fearing we'll be caught in a lie. I needed evidence and facts. These are after all the things the West prides itself on: Numbers. Scientific research. Statistics.

I stepped on the stage next to the Speaker of Parliament and the organizer of the event and said: "I just have one quick thing to say."

I quoted numbers: the death toll in Gaza as well as the growing rate of famine. I was booed. I raised my voice slightly above the heckling and stayed calm. "I promise

I won't take up more than three minutes of your time." I asked that we consider that we are sitting in one of the most powerful rooms in all of Canada. This means we are in a position to change what's happening. "Let us think deeply about how we hold that power."

I continued: "The time will come when the world will apologize for these atrocities, when we will be asked what we did with the power we hold at this moment in history, as witnesses. This is the night for us to start thinking deeply about what our answer to that question will be."

There were more boos, then a yell from the back: "Nazi go home!"

After I finished, I walked off the stage and over to my table, where the mood was icy. Before I could sit down, I was approached by large men with earpieces, telling me to get all my things and follow them out of the room immediately.

I was trying to get my bearings when the organizer of Politics and the Pen walked up to me, stunned and furious. "You stood right next to me, and you didn't say anything. You were *invited*..." his voice trailed off. He stopped himself, then turned and ordered security to "Hurry up, get her out of here."

I recognized the disgust on his face and knew the roots of his rage. It was the same expression as that of the examiner at the University of Cape Town, fuming for the same reason: my ingratitude. How could I fail to recognize the privilege that comes with being only one of a few invited? How could I feel anything but lucky? How could I say anything other than *Thank you*?

We hear this over and over in the West: That we have been rescued from "uncivilized" lands and taken into a more modern and safer world. The event organizer was angry not only because I had spoken of children dying at a time when acknowledging the genocide was taboo, but also because my speech was a show of ingratitude. He was livid. Above all, he was insulted.

We are expected to feel relieved that we are not *"out there with them,"* as my examiner had put it. And our silence must be an expression of that gratitude. Our resistance is seen as insolence, insanity even. And the cure for insanity can only be severe punishment. We must be brought under control. We must be thrown out of rooms we'd been invited into. We must lose our jobs, have invitations revoked, be blacklisted, have our civil liberties violated. Because we are ungrateful.

In my first year at the University of Cape Town I was told that admitting Indigenous African students was "bringing down the university's standards." At my first Politics and the Pen Gala, a famous Giller winner was sure they'd never met me because I was not "one of the usual invited writers." Our place in these spaces will always be tenuous. This is in no small part because our presence is a reminder of past resistance movements. We are walking proof of the triumph of voices of dissent.

I had lived to see the end of apartheid in South Africa, where everyone was either a denier or an agent of resistance. When democracy came, the story was that no one had stood by and done *nothing.* Stories of what people did when witnessing violence can change with the times, like when they are being questioned about where they stood while children were being killed and mass graves were being uncovered. People suddenly either didn't know about apartheid or they had always been against it. Same for the Holocaust. It will be the same for Gaza.

I am an Indigenous person and to be Indigenous anywhere in the world is to be a survivor of genocide. This is true of any Palestinian who has lived past the birth of Israel. It is true of Indigenous peoples who are alive in the Americas. In Aotearoa. Our people were nearly eradicated from our lands. Our lands were taken under force and through bloodshed. But here we stand.

What should we feel lucky for, and to whom do we owe our gratitude? When we look back, will it have been important for us to have stayed in these rooms where silence was the price of admission? Will we be the ones saying we were always against this genocide, conveniently erasing that actually we had said nothing? I was raised by the Biko generation. The message was always: We owe our survival to resistance movements that came before us. To quote an anti-apartheid slogan I grew up with: "An injury to one is an injury to all." Knowing that people stood in protest so that I might live in a world free of bullets and bombs, that my survival mattered to someone back there, *that* is what makes me feel lucky and grateful. Protest is my way of saying *Thank you*.

More than that, protest is an expression of love. It is a way of letting future generations know that their lives were in our hearts. It is a way of telling people in war zones that they are kin. That they are *ours*, that they are *us*.

People speak of generational wealth as passing down money. But generational wealth is also love: the weight of it, the holding of it. The forceful, unbridled expression of it when it matters the most.

My job in these times is to remind the world that Palestinians are our relatives and that we fight for our own. Because when all this ends, we are the ancestors our descendants will look to and ask: What did you do with the power you had at the time? And how did you let me know you loved me?

As I said to everyone in the room that night: Now is a very good time to think about what our answer to these questions will be.

Amy Blanding, right, and Vash Ebbadi-Cook
at the Vancouver Court House, October 2024.
Photo: Michelle Gamage, The Tyee

CHAPTER 23

Sing for Palestine

Amy Blanding

The following incidents took place between April and December 2024. I am going to do my best to avoid embellishment when I tell this story. First, because I will be cross-examined when the associated lawsuits go to court in 2026, and what I say between now and then carries weight for the defense. But more importantly, the absurdity of what occurred needs no embellishment. I want you to see for yourself how easy it is for rights to be stripped away in Canada, no matter what privilege you carry or how secure you may feel. As my favourite tweet about this whole ordeal stated, "Dawg, they're going after white women named 'Bland'—truly no one is safe from Zionists."

I have been an active musician in the British Columbia music scene for over 10 years; the majority of my music is political in nature. I write and sing about migrant rights, disability justice, Missing and Murdered Indigenous Women and Girls, ecosystem collapse, queer liberation, and dismantling the patriarchy. On April 6, 2024, I played a community concert with the Prince George Cantata Singers, a collaboration to profile a local choir and a local singer/songwriter. At the event I sang "Sunbirds," a song I wrote about longing for peace and freedom in Palestine. At the concert's dress rehearsal, I wore a shirt that showed the outline of the shape of occupied Palestine filled in with a watermelon, a symbol that expresses solidarity with the people of Palestine. The shirt was purchased from the organization Wear the Peace, with sale proceeds allocated to aid in Gaza. The night of the concert, I did not wear that shirt or mention Palestine, Hamas, Jews, or genocide.

After the event, I posted on my personal social media page:

> On Saturday, April 6, Reckless Burning and I played a beautiful show in collaboration with the PG Cantata Singers. If you were there, I hope you felt what we all did on stage: musicians of different genres coming together to share the joy of music, storytelling, and the gift of art to a wider audience. I am grateful for the opportunity and proud of the performance. I'm also incredibly grateful to the female-identifying folks who sang "Rise and Agitate" with me.
>
> What you didn't see was that, 10 days prior to the show, I was told by the board of Cantata that my music—in particular, a new song about the genocide in Palestine—was "too divisive," "political," and "highly contentious." Despite being asked not to play these songs, I did so anyway. Divisive is complacency as Israel murders 33,300 civilians, over 14,000 of them children. Political is using starvation as a weapon of war. Contentious is my government complicit in the crush of humanity we are witnessing every hour of every day. The stage is a privilege. I have a responsibility as an artist to use my voice to amplify others and to shine a fierce light on injustice. I will not be censored. We are none of us free until ALL OF US ARE FREE.

The statistics referenced in my post had been corroborated by the International Court of Justice, the United Nations, and others concerning civilian deaths in Gaza and the use of starvation as a tool of war.

These events occurred outside of work, on my personal time. At the time of the concert, I had been working for the Northern Health Authority (one of five health authorities in British Columbia) for close to seven years. I was the Director of Inclusion, Diversity, Equity & Accessibility (IDEA) since August 2023, the first full-time director to hold that position at Northern Health (NH).

On April 24, Northern Health received a letter signed by 11 members (who I will not name for legal reasons) of the Prince George community. In extremely defamatory terms, the signatories demanded that Northern Health take action against me on the basis of my song, my Instagram post, and my T-shirt worn during the rehearsal.

In the factually incorrect, hate-filled, and deeply troubling letter, it was alleged that my song was "Pro-Hamas/Pro-Palestinian and Anti-Israel/Antisemitic"; that my clothing conveyed an "association" with the "Jihadist movement"; that by wearing the T-shirt, I had made a "blatant, visual call for genocide" against the citizens of Israel; that I am "concerned exclusively with atrocities committed by Jews"; and that I have "no concern" for human rights abuses committed elsewhere, such as in Sudan and Ukraine.

The letter went on to accuse me of "hateful, ignorant rants"; that I "directed hatred" at a racial, national, religious or ethnic group; that I "direct [my] attacks exclusively at Jews," "act out of bigotry," and am not able to "deal respectfully and fairly with other minorities." It further asserted that I showed a "total failure to carry out the kind of research in which a person in [my] position is obligated to engage" and that I do not "enquire and think carefully before speaking." The final paragraph of the letter reads:

> We are copying this letter to Nico Slobinsky, Vice President, Pacific Region, of the Centre for Israel and Jewish Affairs and are engaging with other Jewish Civil Rights groups, making them aware of the situation in our community. If Ms. Blanding's behaviour persists, we will not hesitate to take further action. We appreciate your prompt and resolute attention to this matter. Please feel free to contact the undersigned and/or the Jewish Community of Prince George if any clarifications are desired.

On May 7, I was called to a meeting with Northern Health's Vice President Human Resources, David Williams, and my supervisor Vash Ebbadi-Cook, Executive Director, Workforce Sustainability, Quality & Innovation. I was given a few minutes to read the letter from the community members, after which I was subject to an hour-long "interview" where I was required to answer questions not about the validity of the letter, the stated complaints, or our approach as a health authority to other complaints from disgruntled community members. Rather I was required to state what I was prepared to do to ensure that my actions did not compromise the objectives of the IDEA portfolio. It was made clear that I "would need to take steps to rehabilitate the office of IDEA and to ensure that no community group felt unwelcome or unsafe as a result of [my] actions, comments and publications."

I participated in this discussion openly and in good faith. Although I was not given the time or space to respond to the validity of the letter's contents, I explicitly said that "the majority of the statements in this letter are factually incorrect" and "it should go without saying but I will say it anyway: I am not antisemitic." I also expressed very real concerns about my safety, my family's safety, and the safety of other staff at NH who were vocal in their support for Palestine. I asked if the letter had been brought to the NH legal team or if any work had been done relative to ensuring safety given the threats of "further action." This had not occurred to David Williams. I asked that it be prioritized.

On May 10, I was called into another meeting, this time with David Williams and another HR team member, under the assumption that it was in follow-up to the safety concerns I had raised. Instead, David Williams demanded that I publish a pre-drafted statement on my personal social media to apologize and acknowledge that my actions had negatively impacted community members and caused them to feel less safe accessing healthcare services, specifically the Jewish community. The statement went against my political and ethical beliefs. Taken off guard, I did not refuse or agree to the demand; instead, I asked for time to reflect and consider what was being asked of me. I was denied and immediately removed from my position as director of IDEA. The official letter given to me from Northern Health states:

> While you may have intended to express sympathy for the plight of one side of the conflict, the language used in your postings and the wearing of the T-shirt in support of the elimination of the state of Israel, resulted in a community group feeling ostracized and unwelcome. That result is entirely inconsistent with objectives of the Office of IDEA. Finally, you refused to take rehabilitative steps to repair the consequence of your actions.

One week following this meeting, I learned that Vash Ebbadi-Cook had resigned from his position in protest of my removal. To my knowledge, the rationale for my removal or Vash's resignation has not to this day been formally communicated to any NH staff, medical staff, volunteers, or other partners. This and all previous actions beg the questions: Why this case? Why Palestine? What was it that caused Northern Health to completely bypass all appropriate policy, process, and due diligence?

As the implications of my situation became clear, I was able to contact the Palestinian Legal Referral Service, an organization connecting individuals facing repercussions at the workplace for expressing views in support of Palestine and Palestinians with experienced legal counsel. Through this group I acquired legal representation, and on October 9 I filed two lawsuits: the first against Northern Health for wrongful dismissal, defamation, and violation of my Charter rights. The second for defamation against the 11 community members who wrote the original letter. I livestreamed the press conference on the steps of the Vancouver Courthouse, supported by members of Independent Jewish Voices, the BC Civil Liberties Association, physicians, nurses and other healthcare workers and advocates.

At the time of my removal, I was the primary breadwinner in my family. I have a disability that costs between $500 and $1,000 a month in medical supplies. The financial repercussions of my removal, and the implications for my career, are significant. The unfounded accusations of discrimination against me, the ongoing harassment and messages of hate I continue to receive (calling me "a DEI leech," a "sick-ass hypocrite," and saying that "a burka would suit me better than a keffiyeh," that I support terrorism, and direct messages to fellow musicians and bookers in the music industry warning them not to work with me), and the wider implications of what this means in the fight for justice, have deeply impacted my mental and physical health. My concern for my personal safety, my family's safety, and the safety of my friends and former NH colleagues who are outspoken in their support for Palestinian human rights has caused extreme stress and anxiety.

However, I stand firm in my integrity and my rights. Northern Health is one in a long line of organizations who have utterly failed their employees. My job as the director of IDEA was to work to actively dismantle intersecting systems of oppression that perpetuate harm and inequity in the healthcare system, both for employees as well as the patients and families that we serve. Amidst the current health and human resource crisis, this work could not be more critical. I was proud of, and very good at, my job. I grieve every day the good work we were doing to build trust in my community, and how so much of that has been stalled or lost completely. I have deep fear about the increased anti-Arab and Islamophobic sentiments this has perpetuated in the North, and the harmful impacts on the various diasporas who call this place home.

Refusing to be silenced or censored, I went into the recording studio with my band Reckless Burning to record the song "Sunbirds."[1] Released on January 31, 2025, the song is a testament to the unwavering strength and commitment of the people of Palestine, and in solidarity with the struggle across the globe for peace, justice, and freedom from oppression. Every download purchase of "Sunbirds" is directly donated to Wear the Peace for food, water, and aid to Gaza including evacuations for medical surgeries outside of Gaza.

My privilege affords me an incredible opportunity to speak up about what happened, and to hopefully catalyze change within the healthcare system, in my community, and in the greater collective struggle against the rise of fascism. I fundamentally support the right for all people, Jewish and Palestinian included, to live lives free from oppression. We must all be able to rely on our essential Charter rights of freedom of expression.

Note

1. "Sunbirds—Amy Blanding with Reckless Burning," Amy Blanding, YouTube.com/@amyblanding7001, January 2025.

Sunbirds

Music and Lyrics by Amy Blanding

A hot wind blows in February
Last year's fires burning underground
Seasons played the draw, hold fast to something steady
Elevate the children to the clouds

Lord, what of the promise that you made me?
Hold my brothers in arms till the end
Press spices to the meat at the table of my family
Will you ever draw your line in the sand?

Leaves weep oil, first year to miss the harvest
A thousand hands protect a thousand trees
A people born to light are buried in the darkness
But don't forget that all of them are seeds

Sunbirds cry with shame to the land of plenty
Green turns to red turns to brown
Rebels make love in the shells of the city
You don't have to feel your legs to stand your ground

Let this not be ordinary
How can martyred children ever win?
When the trial runs out I know that they will outlive me
Can I make peace with the person that I've been?

Deep, breathe deep, no air is coming
Ashes on the ground
Violent skies, the kites are falling down

You've picked your land, you've staked your winnings
Trappings all around
Mothers wail their babies silent shrouds

Don't confuse famine as hunger for surrender
You can't bomb the fighter out of me
You can censor every song, but we rise up together
One stage one voice till all of us are free

Contributors

Sheima Benembarek is a Moroccan Canadian journalist, writer, and magazine publishing professional, currently a contributing writer for the *Walrus*. Her work has appeared in the *Walrus, Literary Review of Canada, Maisonneuve, Quill & Quire, Chatelaine, Broadview,* and *Vogue Arabia,* focusing on social justice, immigrant narratives, and intersectional feminism. She previously held editorial and business roles at *Strategy, Toronto Life, The Walrus, Corporate Knights,* and *Broadview.* She holds an MFA in creative nonfiction journalism from the University of King's College. Her first book, *Halal Sex: The Intimate Lives of Muslim Womxn in North America* (Penguin Random House, 2023), was shortlisted for the QWF Concordia First Book Prize. She was named an RBC Taylor Prize Emerging Writer in 2020 and served as the Asper Fellow in Media at Western University in 2024.

Abigail B. Bakan is Professor in the Department of Social Justice in Education (SJE), at the Ontario Institute for Studies in Education (OISE), cross-appointed to the Department of Political Science, and an affiliate with the Anne Tanenbaum Centre for Jewish Studies at the University of Toronto. Her research is in the area of anti-oppression politics, with a focus on intersections of gender, race, class, political economy, and citizenship. With Yasmeen Abu-Laban, she is editor of *Human Rights and the United Nations: Paradox and Promise,* and author of *Israel, Palestine and the Politics of Race: Exploring Identity and Power in a Global Context.* Other publications include: *Theorizing Anti-Racism: Linkages in Marxism and Critical Race Theories* (co-edited with Enakshi Dua). She serves on the steering committee of the Jewish Faculty Network.

Amy Blanding (she/her) is a queer, disabled immigrant and settler living on stolen Lheidli T'enneh territory, also known as Prince George, British Columbia. She is a mother and wife with a working-class upbringing and is heavily involved in community and arts-based activism and organizing. With a background in education, facilitation, and leadership development, Amy helps to cultivate workspaces that are safe, trauma-informed, diverse, accessible, fulfilling, and transformational. Amy has been an active musician in British Columbia for over a decade. Known for her profound songwriting, powerful voice, and electric stage presence, she collects moments in the Northern wild and turns them into stalwart, protest folk songs with a raw edge. Boasting collaborations with the Prince George Symphony Orchestra, Kym Gouchie, Rachelle van Zanten, Marcel Gagnon, Reckless Burning, and countless other artists, Amy's music seamlessly bridges the gap between audience, artist, and advocacy toward a greater possibility for the collective.

Safa Chebbi is a decolonial activist and master's candidate in sociology at the University of Quebec in Montreal (UQAM), Safa Chebbi's research interests focus on urban violence, stigmatization, and subalternization. She is a member of the Solidarity for Palestinian Human Rights group at the University of Quebec in Montreal (SDHPP-UQAM), a student group in solidarity with Palestine.

Yara Coussa, a community organizer, immigrated with their family to Montreal from Beirut, Lebanon, at the age of 13. Yara graduated from McGill University in International

Development & Gender Studies, and is currently an intervention worker specialized in care for autistic adults as well as a bookseller at the queer feminist bookstore l'Euguélionne. Yara seeks to create safer spaces for queer, SWANA (South West Asian and North African), and trans people through their involvement with Helem Montréal, La Wild Pride, and other organizations.

Libby Davies has been a social activist for 45-plus years and began as a community organizer in Vancouver's Downtown Eastside in 1972. She was elected to Vancouver City Council for five consecutive terms, 1982-93. As the Member of Parliament for Vancouver East for six consecutive terms, 1997-2015, she became the federal New Democratic Party (NDP) House Leader, (2003-11) and Deputy Leader of the party (2007-15). Libby has been an outspoken advocate for human rights, housing, peace, and social justice throughout her political life. She is currently the co-host of the "Off The Hill" live political panel with rabble.ca. Davies was named to the Order of Canada in 2016, and received the City of Vancouver Civic Merit Award in November 2018. Libby was appointed to the board of governors of Vancouver Community College in 2018. She is also a board member of Canadians for Justice and Peace in the Middle East (CJPME). In May 2022, Libby received the YWCA Woman of Distinction Award.

Duha Elmardi is a Sudanese organizer currently based in Tiohtiàke/Montreal. She is a member of the Sudan Solidarity Collective and supports a number of groups and organizations working toward social and climate justice.

Dr. Yipeng Ge is a primary care physician and public health practitioner based on the traditional, unceded, and unsurrendered territory of the Algonquin Anishinaabeg. In his clinical practice, he works in family medicine and refugee health at a community health centre. He has worked on and studied the structural and colonial determinants of health in both the settler colonial contexts of so-called Canada and occupied Palestine.

Elise Gravel is a well-known and much-loved children's author in Quebec and around the world. She has published dozens of picture books and graphic novels in both English and French. Some of Gravel's books have faced challenges, particularly *Pink, Blue and You! / Le rose, le bleu et toi!*, which was removed from American libraries and schools in February 2022, due to its discussion of gender identity and stereotypes.

Katherine Grzejszczak has been involved in anti-racism and labour activism for over 20 years. She was hired as a Paramedic with York Region in 2010 and graduated from University of Toronto with an undergraduate Sociology degree in 2016. In 2018 Katherine completed Advanced Care Paramedic training through her employer. She was elected president of CUPE Local 905 immediately after and served in that role until 2025. In early 2025 her bargaining unit voted to separate from CUPE 905 and formed the new CUPE Local 4900. Katherine was re-training to return to a front-line ambulance when she was abruptly terminated in June 2025. She is awaiting her grievance arbitration hearing and hopes to be reinstated to her paramedic position with York Region.

Health Workers Alliance for Palestine (HAP) is a group of health workers and learners who have come together in solidarity with Palestine and the Palestinian people driven by principles of social and environmental justice and liberation of oppressed people everywhere. HAP includes Palestinians and allies of different ethnic, cultural, and religious backgrounds.

Yara Jamal is an award-winning Palestinian journalist and writer. Jamal is the founder of Free Palestine Halifax, the largest grassroots organization in Atlantic Canada advocating for Palestinian self-determination, sovereignty, and the right of return. Her work focuses on Palestine and the broader Middle East. Her reporting on the Eskasoni Fish and Wildlife Commission and Indigenous Protected and Conserved Areas (IPCAs) earned her a Gold award from the Canadian Online Publishing Awards. Jamal's work focuses on Middle Eastern politics and structural racism, with a focus on amplifying the voices of marginalized communities.

Iman Kassam is Canadian broadcast journalist with over 14 years of experience in radio, television, podcasting, and digital media. They have reported extensively on Indigenous issues, working with Native Communications and APTN National News before moving to CBC Radio and CTV News Montreal. Their work is rooted in ethical journalism and community engagement, shaped by nearly a decade covering devolution, land claims, land and water rights, and language revitalization. Iman's SSHRC-funded Master's research explores how Generation Z Canadians determine trust and credibility in the news, alongside research projects on mis/disinformation and the online harassment of journalists.

Thoby King is a white Toronto-based settler, a lawyer, a writer and an activist. He works in the legal clinic system and runs an independent activist legal practice.

Nora Loreto is a writer and activist based in Quebec City. She has written five books and countless articles about Canadian politics and social movements. She is the president of the Canadian Freelance Union and editor with the Canadian Association of Labour Media. Along with Sandy Hudson, she hosts the popular podcast *Sandy and Nora Talk Politics.*

Ehab Lotayef is a Canadian poet, writer, community activist, and IT Manager of Egyptian origin. He holds a degree in electrical engineering (1981) from Ain-Shams University in Cairo, Egypt. He moved to Canada in 1989 and has worked at McGill University since 1999. He published a bilingual poetry collection, *To Love a Palestinian Woman* (TSAR) in 2010, while the CBC produced his play *Crossing Gibraltar* in 2006. Ehab is deeply involved in social and community work, including campaigns against the sanctions and war on Iraq, opposing the blockade of Gaza (organizing and being on board the Freedom Flotilla) and advocating for Indigenous rights. He is also a founder and former chairperson of both Muslim Awareness Week (MAW) and the Non à la loi 21 (#NL21) campaign. Ehab is a founder and coordinator of the Montreal dialogue group Kalemat (meaning "words"), a freethinkers' forum aiming to advocate open dialogue, in particular among those originating from Arabic-speaking countries.

Hunaifa Malik is a PhD candidate in political science at McGill University. Her writing centers on an ethnographic study on pro-Palestine demonstrations in Montreal, and the intersections of identity and the right to protest in Canada.

Leila Marshy is the author of *The Philistine* (LLP, 2018) and *My Thievery of the People* (Baraka Books, 2025). Daughter of a Palestinian refugee to Canada, Marshy lived in Cairo during the first Intifada and worked for the Palestinian Red Crescent; in Gaza, for the Palestinian Mental Health Association; and in Montreal for Medical Aid for Palestine. She has been a community and political organizer, including founding a dialogue group with the Hasidic community in her neighbourhood and, as campaign manager, helping elect the first Hasidic woman to political office in the world. Marshy is Editor at Baraka Books and lives in Montreal.

Samira Mohyeddin is editor-in-chief and founder of *On the Line Media* (*OTL*), a digital journalism organization. A former CBC Radio host and producer, she doesn't shy away from identifying as a queer reporter from Iran or withhold critiques of traditional news media. A true multi-talent, Mohyeddin has a background in theatre studies from the American Musical and Dramatic Academy in New York City. She completed her undergraduate degree in religion and later earned a master's degree in gender and modern Middle Eastern history from the University of Toronto. In 2023, she quit CBC to start *OTL*—and the rest is history.

Kagiso Lesego Molope is an Indigenous South African Canadian novelist and playwright. Born and raised in South Africa, Kagiso Lesego Molope graduated from the University of Cape Town and moved to Canada at age 21. Her first novel, *Dancing in the Dust* (Mawenzi House, 2002), was the first novel by an Indigenous South African author to be on the IBBY List. In 2015, she was the first Black author to win the Percy FitzPatrick Award, and the first Black novelist to win the Ottawa Book Award in 2019. That same year, Molope won the Pius Adesanmi Memorial Award for her book *Such A Lovely, Lonely Road* (Mawenzi House, 2018). McClelland & Stewart has acquired world rights to her fifth novel *We Inherit the Fire.*

Mo Pareles is associate professor of English at the University of British Columbia. They are a graduate of Yale and New York Universities and the author of *Nothing Pure: Jewish Law, Christian Supersession, and Bible Translation in Old English* (University of Toronto Press, 2024). Mo is a founding member of the UBC chapter of the Jewish Faculty Network.

Robin Philpot is Publisher of Baraka Books and the author of seven books in French and English. He was president of the Quebec-Palestine Committee in the 1980s. He lives in Montreal.

Arfa Rana is a Pakistani-Canadian journalist who previously worked with CBC in New Brunswick and London, Ontario, before resigning in June 2024 in protest of CBC's complicity in genocide. She completed a Master's in International Public Policy at Wilfrid Laurier University in 2025 with specialization in human security and global migration. Her reporting and analysis have appeared in *Mondoweiss, Electronic Intifada, CBC, Geo News,* and *The Analyst News*. For updates, follow her on X @arfadorable.

Jillian Rogin, BA Hons (Trent University), MES (York University), LLB (University of Windsor), LLM (Osgoode Hall, York University), PhD student (Osgoode Hall, York University) is an Associate Professor at the University of Windsor, Faculty of Law and a criminal defence lawyer. Her research interests include criminal law, legal clinic scholarship, critical race/anti-colonial theory, and critical Jewish studies. Jillian is an active member of Independent Jewish Voices (IJV), Jewish Voice for Peace (JVP), Faculty 4 Palestine, and the Jewish Faculty Network (JFN). Her PhD research focuses on pro-Israel advocacy in the enactment of hate speech legislation in Canada including changing conceptions of antisemitism over time.

Sean Tucker is a professor (part-time) in the faculty of business administration at the University of Regina and a sessional lecturer at the UBC School of Population and Public Health. His primary areas of teaching and research are 1) worker health and safety and 2) leadership. He is a member of Faculty 4 Palestine at UBC and the University of Regina.

Lesley Wood is a Professor of Sociology at York University. She does research on social movements and policing, and was arrested as one of the Indigo 11.

Anna Zalik is Professor of Environmental and Urban Change at York University. Her research concerns the oil, gas, and mining industries on which she has published and presented widely. Zalik has been active in Palestine solidarity work since the early 1990s, including in Faculty4Palestine, and is a founding and steering committee member of the Jewish Faculty Network.

APPENDIX I

Boycott, divestment, sanctions

BDSmovement.net

(i) Organization Summary

The Boycott, Divestment, Sanctions (BDS) movement works to end international support for Israel's oppression of Palestinians. It was launched in 2005 by 170 Palestinian unions, refugee networks, women's organizations, professional associations, popular resistance committees, and other Palestinian civil society bodies as a form of non-violent protest. It operates through BDSmovement.net as its official website and is led by the Palestinian BDS National Committee.

Inspired by the South African anti-apartheid movement, the Palestinian BDS calls for non-violent pressure on Israel until it complies with international law by meeting three demands:

1. **Ending Israel's occupation and colonization of all Arab lands and dismantling the illegal apartheid wall.** This includes ending the occupation of territories captured in 1967 and dismantling what BDS refers to as the "West Bank barrier wall."

2. **Full equality for Palestinian citizens of present-day Israel.** This calls for "recognizing the fundamental rights of the Arab-Palestinian citizens of Israel to full equality," addressing what the movement sees as discriminatory treatment of Palestinian citizens within Israel proper.
3. **The right of return for Palestinian refugees.** This involves "respecting, protecting, and promoting the rights of Palestinian refugees to return to their homes and properties as stipulated in UN resolution 194."

(ii) Tactics and Impact

The BDS movement employs multiple strategic approaches including consumer boycotts, institutional divestment campaigns, and pressure for governmental sanctions. The calls to divest have increasingly forced enterprises to avoid Israeli companies, investors to withhold capital, and banks and pension funds to not invest consumer money in Israel. The boycott of companies affiliated with Zionist Israel has become a global phenomenon, significantly impacting numerous major corporations worldwide. Some examples of BDS successes include:

- Ben & Jerry's ended their business partnership with Israel.
- SodaStream closed its West Bank production facility.
- Telecommunications company Orange cut ties with its Israeli licensee.
- French multinational Veolia sold its Israeli water, waste, and energy interests.
- Several singers and artists have cancelled their appearances in Israel including Lauryn Hill, Elvis Costello, Lana Del Ray, Lorde, and more.
- The Giller Prize ended its ties with its largest funder, Scotiabank, which in turn divested half its stake from the Israeli arms manufacturer Elbit Systems.

- In October 2024, more than 1,000 authors worldwide, including Canadians Miriam Toews, Leanne Betasamosake Simpson, and Dionne Brand, signed a letter pledging to boycott Israeli cultural institutions.[1]

(iii) Criticism and Controversy

Critics argue that the BDS movement threatens and delegitimizes the state of Israel. In 2019, the German Parliament passed a symbolic non-binding resolution declaring BDS antisemitic and that it was "reminiscent of the most terrible chapter in German history."[2]

Its lack of measurable impact has led some detractors to say BDS is little more than symbolic, and has not achieved the movement's core goals, such as ending the occupation or ensuring Palestinian refugees' right of return

Notes

1. Asma Sahebzada, "Canadian authors including Miriam Toews and Rupi Kaur sign open letter to boycott Israeli cultural institutions," *Toronto Star*, 3 March 2025.
2. "Germany labels Israel boycott movement BDS antisemitic," BBC, 17 May 2019.

APPENDIX II

Canary Mission

CanaryMission.com

(i) Organization Summary

Canary Mission is an anonymously run website established in 2015 to document people and groups who purportedly promote hatred of Israel and Jews on college campuses in the USA and Canada. The organization's detailed profiles and dossiers are publicly available online and intended for wide use. Canary Mission has been known to actively send these profiles to employers and the media. Despite its secretive nature, investigative reporting[1] has revealed that the operation is directed from Israel and funded by wealthy Americans and Jewish American foundations, with documented funding sources including major Jewish community foundations.[2]

(ii) Tactics and Impact

Canary Mission has been described as a literal blacklist that works by maintaining a massive doxxing operation. The organization's tactics have had significant real-world consequences, with people tracked by Canary Mission saying they've experienced anxiety and found themselves stepping back from pro-Palestine advocacy as a result.[3] In some cases, the organization has claimed credit for more severe consequences, including the deportation in the US targeting of Tufts graduate student Rumeysa Ozturk, suggesting their profiles may influence government actions.

Canary Mission lists extend beyond current students to individuals in their professional careers. The organization's practice of sending profiles to employers[4] means that students and faculty may face employment difficulties or professional retaliation long after their university involvement in pro-Palestinian activism.[5]

(iii) Criticism and Concerns

Canary Mission has faced substantial criticism from academic and civil liberties communities. Critics have described Canary Mission as weaponizing the accusation of antisemitism in order to silence critique of Israel, with some comparing its methods to McCarthyite tactics and employing open racism.[6] The Middle East Studies Association's Committee on Academic Freedom has issued a resource guide[7] for college and university leaders on actions they can take to counteract the secretive Canary Mission, viewing it as a threat to academic freedom. Critics argue that Canary Mission operates as "the most significant and effective pro-Israel intimidation tool" that "operates 24/7 and constantly updates its targets," raising serious concerns about the chilling effect on legitimate academic discourse and political expression on university campuses.

Notes

1. James Bamford, "Who is Funding Canary Mission? Inside the Doxxing Operation Targeting Anti-Zionist Students and Professors," *The Nation*, 22 December 2023.
2. Alex Kane, "Canary Mission's Newest Funders," *Jewish Currents*, 4 April 2025.
3. Margaret Ferguson, David Simpson, "Educators need to denounce the smear tactics of Canary Mission," *Mondoweiss*, 25 February 2018.

4. Zack Beauchamp, "This pro-Israel group keeps a blacklist. Now it's taking credit for deportations," *Vox*, 25 April 2025.
5. "Exposing Canary Mission: A Resource for College and University Leaders," Committee on Academic Freedom, Middle East Studies Association of North America.
6. Professor L. Ali Khan, "Academic Freedom Under Attack: The Chilling Effect of Surveillance Sites on US Professors Who Criticize Israel," *JuristNews*, 20 November 2023.
7. "Exposing Canary Mission: A Resource for College and University Leaders," Committee on Academic Freedom, Middle East Studies Association of North America.

APPENDIX III

Hasbara

Israel's Public Diplomacy Strategy

(i) Summary

Hasbara was developed in the early 20th century as a propaganda strategy to craft a controlled narrative of Israel. Meaning "explanation" in Hebrew, Hasbara is used to bolster home front unity, ensure the support of allies, disrupt efforts to organize hostile coalitions, determine how issues are defined by the media and social networks, establish parameters of politically correct discourse, delegitimize critics and their arguments, and shape common understanding of international negotiations. A core Hasbara approach is to present Israel and the Jewish people as eternal victims and therefore in need of staunch support and aggressive defense.

Hasbara has evolved significantly with digital technology, giving rise to what is being called Hasbara 2.0—the use of social media and digital platforms by the Israeli state and supporters in order to increase pro-Israel sentiments worldwide.

(ii) Tactics and Methods

The Hasbara strategy is a blend of diplomatic efforts, mainstream media influence, and modern digital engagement. Government-coordinated messaging flows through official channels, such as the IDF Spokesperson's Unit and Prime Minister's office, while cultural diplomacy initiatives work to present Israel in a positive light, demonstrating the country's broader cultural, technological, and social contributions.

Simultaneously, sophisticated digital operations involve content production across social media platforms, media houses, and lobbying efforts, including comprehensive training programs that prepare official representatives and grassroots supporters to engage in online advocacy and campaigns designed to shape discourse across digital platforms.

The objective is to control how issues are framed, with particular emphasis on delegitimizing critics and building counter-narratives. By establishing the parameters of discussion and discourse, Hasbara aims to prevent the formation of hostile coalitions against Israeli policies. During the second Intifada, for example, Israel began circulating pictures of Palestinian children, some of them babies, as terrorists with bombs hidden in their clothing. These images were proven to be false.[1] More recently, the lies about dead babies, "pregnant women being disemboweled, and Israeli children kept in cages" on October 7, 2023, were typical of Hasbara strategy.[2]

(iii) Budget and spending

The Hasbara budget has recently increased by $150 million, representing a dramatic escalation in funding that took effect in late 2024/early 2025, indicating Israel's recognition of the need for significantly enhanced public diplomacy efforts.[3] The surge in spending comes as Israel's public image is sagging around the world over the onslaught in Gaza.

It is one of the most significant investments in state-sponsored public diplomacy efforts by any country, reflecting both the perceived importance of the information war and Israel's substantial financial commitment to shaping international public opinion.

Notes

1. "Argument over baby's picture," Dawn.com, 29 June 2002.
2. Alain Gresh, "Hasbara: the dark art of spinning a war," *Le Monde Diplomatique*, May 2024.
3. "Foreign ministry to receive massive budget for public diplomacy," *Times of Israel*, 29 December 2024.

APPENDIX IV

HonestReporting Canada

HonestReporting.ca

(i) Organization Summary

HonestReporting is an American-based media watchdog and advocacy group. It operates in a number of countries, including Canada (HonestReporting Canada), where it enjoys charitable status. Its mission is to combat "ideological prejudice in journalism and the media" against Jews and Israel.

(ii) Tactics and Operations

HonestReporting Canada (HRC) employs coordinated pressure campaigns against Canadian media outlets and journalists for reports and coverage deemed antisemitic or anti-Israel. In many cases, HRC pressures newsrooms beyond factual corrections, urging removals of entire guest segments or op-eds that criticize Israeli policy. Journalists are called out by name on the HRC website, and the over 70,000 members are mobilized to send in pre-written complaint forms, often resulting in sustained campaigns of harassment.

According to a journalist quoted in the independent media site *Converse* and who wished to remain anonymous for fear of reprisal: "Some simply use the model proposed by HRC, but others are personalized with messages like: 'Shame on you,' 'You are spreading Hamas propaganda,' 'You should be fired immediately.' HonestReporting takes the smallest thing, twists it and throws fire at it, it's so ridiculous. Because now everything is antisemitic for them."[1]

In their 2025 first quarter report,[2] HRC claims to have had a hand in "creating some of the most engaging pro-Israel content in the world," counting the *National Post* and Ben Mulroney among their "collaborators." Among their "successes" are hundreds of retractions, apologies, cancellations, and rewrites from such organizations as the *Toronto Star, Globe and Mail, La Presse, Montreal Gazette*, CBC, Radio-Canada, *Calgary Herald*, CTV, *City News, Edmonton Journal, National Post, The Guardian, Winnipeg Sun*, and more. "Every day, The HonestReporting posts two to eight 'action alerts' aimed at one or another of these information actors," says another journalist in the *Converse* article who was targeted and wishes to remain anonymous for fear of reprisal.

In 2022, HRC partnered with Hasbara Canada to create the "Canadian Campus Media Program," designed to monitor campus media and respond to "problematic" coverage. In their Q1 report for 2025, HRC lists 13 college media articles that resulted from their targeted pressure tactics. As of 2023, 23 students from 14 universities have been accepted into the program.[3]

The organization receives significant financial backing. According to an investigative series by *The Maple*, HonestReporting Canada is generously funded by a mix of private family foundations and philanthropic organizations, including individuals and organizations who hold "important positions in a range of industries and fields, including real estate, law, academia, retail, news media, oil, health care, government, banking and finance, and others."[4] Some of the top donors may be familiar to Canadians: the Azrieli Foundation, the Asper Foundation, the Peter and Melanie Munk Charitable Foundation, the Rotman Family Foundation, the Linda Frum and Howard Sokolowski Charitable Foundation, among others.

(iii) Criticism and Impact on Press Freedom

The organization faces substantial criticism from journalists and press freedom advocates who argue its activities constitute harassment and create a chilling effect on reporting. Several Canadian journalists have spoken out, saying they are being pressured, with one award-winning journalist describing feeling "hunted" by HRC.[5] There have also been formal complaints to the Canada Revenue Agency on behalf of "media workers who have been victims of harassment from HonestReporting Canada or similar media lobbies."[6]

While HRC sees itself as a "digital army for Israel," critics note that CBC's repeated caving to a highly biased pro-Israel advocacy group is part of the larger context of right-wing populism on the rise in Canada today. Media scholars and advocacy groups have documented the "chilling effect" on Palestinian reporting, raising concerns about the organization's impact on journalistic independence and the public's access to diverse perspectives on Middle Eastern affairs.[7]

Notes

1. Loubna Chlaikhy, "Investigation: Journalists denounce pressure from the pro-Israel group HonestReporting Canada," *Converse*, 22 October 2024.
2. HonestReporting Canada Impact Report, 2025 1st Quarter Edition, HonestReporting Canada.
3. Ibid.
4. Davide Mastracci, "Meet the Billionaire-Funded Pro-Israel Group Influencing Media," *The Maple*, 29 January 2024.
5. See this volume, "Silence. One Second. Five Seconds," Arfa Rana.
6. Formal Complaint submitted to CRA: HonestReporting Canada, Just Peace Advocates, ActionNetwork.org
7. Alex Cosh, "Journalists Urged to Report Threats Received After Pro-Israel Campaigns," *The Maple*, 24 October 2024.

APPENDIX V

IHRA Working Definition of Antisemitism

HolocaustRemembrance.com

(i) Summary

The IHRA definition of antisemitism is the "non-legally binding working definition of antisemitism" adopted by the International Holocaust Remembrance Alliance (IHRA) in 2016.[1] It was first published in 2005 by the European Monitoring Centre on Racism and Xenophobia (EUMC), a European Union agency. In 2019, the Government of Canada adopted the non-legally binding International Holocaust Remembrance Alliance Working Definition of Antisemitism (IHRA Definition) as part of Canada's Anti-Racism Strategy. As of the date of publication, the IHRA definition has been adopted by 42 other countries and multiple international organizations.

(ii) Controversy

The IHRA definition has generated significant controversy, particularly around its Israel-related examples, which critics argue are used to suppress legitimate criticism of Israeli policies.[2] Academic scholars, including legal experts and Holocaust historians, have raised concerns that the definition conflates antisemitism with anti-Zionism and criticism of Israel, potentially weaponizing antisemitism accusations to stifle free speech in the media, on university campuses, and in political discourse.[3]

(iii) Complete Text

Antisemitism is a certain perception of Jews, which may be expressed as hatred toward Jews. Rhetorical and physical manifestations of antisemitism are directed toward Jewish or non-Jewish individuals and/or their property, toward Jewish community institutions and religious facilities.

To guide IHRA in its work, the following examples may serve as illustrations:

Manifestations might include the targeting of the state of Israel, conceived as a Jewish collectivity. However, criticism of Israel similar to that leveled against any other country cannot be regarded as antisemitic. Antisemitism frequently charges Jews with conspiring to harm humanity, and it is often used to blame Jews for "why things go wrong." It is expressed in speech, writing, visual forms and action, and employs sinister stereotypes and negative character traits.

Contemporary examples of antisemitism in public life, the media, schools, the workplace, and in the religious sphere could, taking into account the overall context, include, but are not limited to:

1. Calling for, aiding, or justifying the killing or harming of Jews in the name of a radical ideology or an extremist view of religion.
2. Making mendacious, dehumanizing, demonizing, or stereotypical allegations about Jews as such or the power

of Jews as a collective—such as, especially but not exclusively, the myth about a world Jewish conspiracy or of Jews controlling the media, economy, government, or other societal institutions.

3. Accusing Jews as a people of being responsible for real or imagined wrongdoing committed by a single Jewish person or group, or even for acts committed by non-Jews.
4. Denying the fact, scope, mechanisms (e.g., gas chambers) or intentionality of the genocide of the Jewish people at the hands of National Socialist Germany and its supporters and accomplices during World War II (the Holocaust).
5. Accusing the Jews as a people, or Israel as a state, of inventing or exaggerating the Holocaust.
6. Accusing Jewish citizens of being more loyal to Israel, or to the alleged priorities of Jews worldwide, than to the interests of their own nations.
7. Denying the Jewish people their right to self-determination, e.g., by claiming that the existence of a State of Israel is a racist endeavour.
8. Applying double standards by requiring of it a behavior not expected or demanded of any other democratic nation.
9. Using the symbols and images associated with classic antisemitism (e.g., claims of Jews killing Jesus or blood libel) to characterize Israel or Israelis.
10. Drawing comparisons of contemporary Israeli policy to that of the Nazis.
11. Holding Jews collectively responsible for actions of the state of Israel.

Antisemitic acts are criminal when they are so defined by law (for example, denial of the Holocaust or distribution of antisemitic materials in some countries).

Criminal acts are antisemitic when the targets of attacks, whether they are people or property—such as buildings, schools, places of worship and cemeteries—are selected because they are, or are perceived to be, Jewish or linked to Jews.

Antisemitic discrimination is the denial to Jews of opportunities or services available to others and is illegal in many countries.

Notes

1. Working definition of antisemitism, International Holocaust Remembrance Alliance.
2. Chris McGreal, "UN urged to reject antisemitism definition over misuse to shield Israel," *The Guardian*, 24 April 2023.
3. "Canada's IHRA Handbook Threatens both Palestinians and Jews," Joint Statement, Independent Jewish Voices, 31 October 2024.

APPENDIX VI

Political Lobbying

AIPAC and Canadian Counterparts

USA: AIPAC

(i) Summary

The American Israel Public Affairs Committee (AIPAC) is widely regarded as one of the most powerful and influential lobbying organizations in Washington, DC, if not the world.[1] Founded in 1963, AIPAC works with both Democratic and Republican officials to maintain robust American support for Israel, including military aid, diplomatic backing, and strategic cooperation. AIPAC maintains that a strong US-Israel partnership serves American strategic interests in the Middle East. The organization has played a significant role in securing billions in annual US aid to Israel, shaping American Middle East policy for decades.

(ii) Tactics and Methods

AIPAC staff regularly meet with members of Congress and their aides to advocate for pro-Israel legislation and oppose measures seen as harmful to Israeli interests. The organization provides detailed policy briefings, talking points, and research, positioning itself as the go-to source for information on the

Middle East. AIPAC's annual Policy Conference brings thousands of activists to Washington, creating a massive lobbying effort. AIPAC works with other pro-Israel groups, Jewish organizations, and Christian Zionist communities. Although it emphasizes its independence as an American organization advocating for American interests, AIPAC maintains strict message discipline and coordinates closely with Israel.

(iii) Budget

AIPAC's substantial budget has grown significantly over the decades; it is currently estimated to be around $100-120 million, funded primarily through membership dues, donations, and fundraising events.[2] AIPAC's financial influence extends beyond its direct lobbying expenditures, spreading out through its network of affiliated political action committees (PACs). In 2021, AIPAC established a super PAC called United Democracy Project, which has spent tens of millions of dollars in federal elections, often targeting candidates perceived as insufficiently supportive of Israel. The organization maintains a large professional staff, conducts extensive research operations, hosts major conferences, and sustains year-round advocacy efforts. When key votes or policy debates emerge, AIPAC's fundraising capabilities enable it to mobilize significant resources quickly.

(iv) Controversies

Critics argue that AIPAC wields disproportionate influence over American foreign policy. The organization has been accused of using its political influence to suppress criticism of Israeli policies and to marginalize voices advocating for Palestinian rights. AIPAC's aggressive campaign spending through affiliated PACs has drawn criticism for targeting prominent members of Congress who have been critical of Israeli policies. The organization has faced scrutiny over its relationship with Israeli intelligence services and faces questions about whether some of its activities should require registration under the Foreign Agents Registration Act (FARA). Additionally, some former AIPAC officials have been involved in espionage-related controversies, and the organization's unwavering support for various Israeli government positions has put it at odds with American diplomatic efforts or broader international consensus.

A growing number of American politicians and candidates are publicly rejecting AIPAC and its agenda. But while encouraging, they represent less than 5% of the total number of sitting members of Congress. Out of 535 members of Congress (435 House + 100 Senate), AIPAC sent more than $53 million to 361 candidates in 2024. This does not include those who may receive other types of AIPAC funding through super PAC spending.

CANADA: CIJA, CJPAC, and B'NAI BRITH CANADA

While Canadian politics does not allow for the kind of political lobbying and money exchange that exists in the United States, there are a handful of organizations in Canada that have similar goals, do similar work, and may have a similar impact.

The Centre for Israel and Jewish Affairs (CIJA) is currently the primary organization that serves as Canada's equivalent to AIPAC. CIJA emerged in 2011 as the leading voice of the Israeli lobby in Canada, taking over from earlier organizations such as the Canada-Israel Committee. CIJA describes itself as "the official representative organizational voice of the Jewish community of Canada" and is highly active in lobbying the Canadian government on Israel-related issues.

The Canadian Jewish Political Affairs Committee (CJPAC) also plays a significant role. CJPAC's leaders have attended each annual AIPAC conference since 2003, and the *Canadian Jewish News* reported that "AIPAC plays an advisory and mentoring role for CIJA-PAC." CJPAC has about 2,000 members, making it almost comparable on a per capita basis to AIPAC.

Alongside its broader human rights mission and community support, **B'nai Brith Canada** operates as a prominent pro-Israel advocacy group and maintains diplomatic relationships that support Israel advocacy. The organization identifies itself as "a staunch defender of the State of Israel and global Jewry" and is committed to "the security and continuity of the Jewish people and the State of Israel." B'nai Brith Canada frames its Israel advocacy within its broader mission of combating antisemitism and protecting Jewish communities, often presenting criticism of Israel as antisemitic in nature.

Independent Jewish Voices has called B'nai Brith Canada's widely quoted documenting of antisemitic incidents as fear-inducing, unreliable, exaggerated, and dangerous.[3]

AIPAC vs CANADA similarities:

- CIJA, CJPAC, and B'nai Brith Canada also lobby government officials on pro-Israel policies.
- They engage in public advocacy and education efforts to encourage and bolster relations with Israel.
- They maintain close ties with Israel and see themselves as sharing the same goals.

AIPAC vs CANADA differences:

- Canadian lobby groups operate in a different political system (parliamentary vs. presidential) and are bound by stricter restrictions, including mandated one to two year "cooling off periods" where lobbyists must step back.
- Lobbyists in Canada are not allowed to give cash, monetary gifts, or anything more than a token to a politician they are currently lobbying or expect to lobby.

- The scale of their efforts are smaller, reflecting Canada's smaller population and narrower sphere of influence.
- The Canadian organizations are less publicly prominent than AIPAC.

Notes

1. Sheryl Gay Stolberg, "Ilhan Omar's Criticism Raises the Question: is AIPAC too Powerful?" *The New York Times*, 4 March 2019.
2. Jake Johnson, "Very bad sign for democracy: AIPAC has spent over $100 million on 2024 elections," *Common Dreams*, 28 August 2024.
3. *The B'nai Brith Audit of Antisemitic Incidents: An Unreliable and Dangerous Document*, Report, Independent Jewish Voices, IJVCanada.org, June 2024.

Earlier versions of the following submissions were previously published, and are reprinted here with permission.

We Must Be Allowed to Speak Out
Gabor Maté, "What is happening in Gaza is an injury to our collective conscience. We must be allowed to speak out," *Toronto Star*, 20 June 2025.

Policing the Window: The Case of the Indigo 11
Thoby King, "The Indigo 11 and Toronto Police's dubious hate crime narrative," Rabble.ca, 5 December 2023.

Uncompromising Solidarity: Struggling for Political Memory
Safa Chebbi, "Solidarités du Coeur de l'Empire," Revue-Ouvrage.org, Translated by Robin Philpot, 10 July 2024,

What Being Pro-Palestinian Means to Me
Sheima Benembarek, "What Being Pro-Palestinian Means to Me," *The Walrus*, 13 February 2024.

Do You See What They See: Gen Z and the New Media
Iman Kassam, "Beyond the Famine Frame," *J-Source*, 14 August 2025.

Statements

No to Weaponizing Antisemitism
Open Letter, "Une deformation du concept d'antisémitisme," *La Presse*, 11 April 2024.

End the Repression in Canada's Health Sector
"End the Repression in Canada's Health Sector," Health WorkersforPalestine.org, 4 May 2025.

Printed by Imprimerie Gauvin
Gatineau, Québec